WORDPRESS E-COMMERCE BLUEPRINT

How to Create and Manage WordPress Online Store for Beginner

Suhaili Shazreena

WordPress E-Commerce Blueprint : How to Create and Manage WordPress Online Store for Beginner

Copyright © 2017 by Suhaili Shazreena

All rights reserved. Printed in the United States of America. No part of this book may be used or reproduced in any manner whatsoever without written permission except in the case of brief quotations em- bodied in critical articles or reviews.

For information contact :
suhaili.shazreena@theefficientyou.com
http://www.theefficientyou.com

Credit to Freepik.com for the vector graphic
ISBN-13: 978-1545338063
ISBN-10: 154533806X

First Edition: April 2017

CONTENTS

A Note to the Reader 1

Chapter 1 6

    Making a Switch to WordPress 6

Chapter 2 20

    Why WordPress? 20

Chapter 3 26

    Registering Your Domain Name 26

Chapter 4 35

    Getting a Hosting Plan for Your Online Store 35

Chapter 5 45

    Turning Your WordPress Site into an Online Store .. 45

Chapter 6 59

    Getting a Premium WordPress Theme for Your Online Store 59

Chapter 7 69

    Accepting Payment at Your Online Store 69

Chapter 8 76

    Getting SSL Certificate for Your Online Store 76

Chapter 9 82

    Creating Email Addresses Specifically for Your Online Store 82

Chapter 10 90

   Other WordPress Plugins You Should Install 90

Chapter 11 102

   Important Pages to Have On Your Online Store 102

Chapter 12 112

   Configuring Shipping Rate for Your Online Store .. 112

Chapter 13 122

   Writing a Product Description That Sells 122

Chapter 14 129

   Managing Your Orders 129

Chapter 15 139

   Shipment Packaging for Your Online Store 139

Chapter 16 148

   Order Fulfillment Service for Your Online Store 148

Chapter 17 162

   Marketing Your Online Store 162

Chapter 18 192

   Outsourcing Tasks for Your Online Store 192

Chapter 19 203

   Bookkeeping Simplified for Your Business 203

Before You Leave 209

Sample Store 211

Resources Mentioned In This Book 213

About The Author 219

A NOTE TO THE READER

You feel skeptical as you pick this book. Well, there are countless books out there, talking about how you can create an online store on your own. But you end up picking this book instead. Of many books available, why this book? You're only curious if it's possible for you to create an online store on WordPress. You already read a lot of books and blogs, talking about creating an online store on your own. But the idea of using WordPress to create an online store seems non-existent to you.

Okay, let me shed this skepticism out of you. Yes, it's possible that you can create an online store on WordPress. If it's your first time hearing about

WordPress or you may hear about it but never try it yourself, then don't worry. WordPress is easy to use, even for a complete beginner. I have no idea how many people I encounter who admit that they're not tech-savvy. But they're doing fine with using WordPress. In fact, they recommend it to their audience.

So, I'm doing the same thing to you. Sure, I love WordPress, and I use WordPress pretty much for everything. But another reason for me to recommend WordPress is that it's cost-effective. You don't need a huge budget to create a professional-looking online store. I'm not saying this out of thin air. I'm saying this because my old online retail store, Fashion Paraizo is on WordPress. Heck, you can't even tell that the store is a WordPress-based online store.

And what's the best part? You can create the online store on your own without hiring people to do it for you. But if you don't have the time to play around with WordPress, then you can always hire someone to do the job for you. Even if you choose to hire someone, you still need to know what you need to create an online store on WordPress. You don't have to be an expert in it. But it can help you to communicate with the web developer better.

But if you're a DIY-er like me and you don't have

a budget to hire someone to do it for you, then this book is perfect for you. I write this book for people who have no technical background and experience. What's even better, the online store won't cost you an arm and a leg. So, you can still create an online store even if you're a complete beginner.

This book not only talks about creating an online store on WordPress. But it's also focusing on building a foundation for your online store management. It covers everything you need to know about managing your online store. And that includes fulfilling your orders and bookkeeping for your business. With this book, you can manage your online store like a pro even if you never manage any business in your entire life. Think of it like having a consultant in a book form.

Now, here's another thing that I like to touch upon. If you happen to be a business resides outside of the US, then don't ditch this book yet. I also include many alternative solutions for businesses outside of the US. So, you can still use what I recommend in this book even if you don't live in the US. I understand how hard it is to find solutions for the international business since I also don't live in the US. Keep in mind that you still need to check if the websites have any country restriction. But for the most part, the solution is available for most countries.

So, who will benefit this book the most? For the apparent reason, it's for people who are selling physical products in a marketplace like eBay. And they're also thinking about having their own online store. You can choose to ditch eBay for good or use eBay as an extension to your online store. If you've decided to remain on eBay, I will also show you how to handle the fulfillment for both stores.

If it's your first time with selling online, then this book is also beneficial to you too. You don't have to start selling on marketplaces like eBay and Amazon Marketplace. You can jump right away and start selling your products in your own online store. If you already know where to source your products, then you're ready to go.

But what if you don't know what to sell on your online store? Should you still pick this book? If this is you, then my suggestion is to do your research first before attempting to create an online store. This book doesn't cover product and niche selection process. So, you need to know what you want to sell beforehand. I write this book in such a way that people who pick this book already know what they want to sell. And they already know what products are selling well online.

Also, I'm going to be honest here that this book can be a bit technical to some people. But I'll do my best to make the explanations as simple as possible without making your head spins. But then again, don't let the technical side of things overwhelm you and prevent you from progressing.

Sure, it can be a bit confusing at first. But I'm sure that you'll get the hang of it if you take the time to get yourself familiarize with WordPress. And you also keep on learning everything you need to know about managing your business. Success will come to you if you put the efforts you need to make it happen.

CHAPTER 1

Making a Switch to WordPress

"You could use WordPress to create an online store? I thought that it was only for blogging," Roald said to me. He was the owner of the fulfillment center in Malaysia. I nodded at him. "Yup, in fact, you could create any websites you want with WordPress." WordPress isn't only for blogging. But for people like Roald, they never thought that WordPress is capable of such things.

I was no different than everyone else when it

comes to WordPress. I know that you can use WordPress as a membership site and a website for lead generations. But using WordPress as an online store? No one had ever told me that it was possible. Sure, I know that some people sell their products and services on their website. But they're all selling services or digital products, not physical products. And their website isn't a full e-commerce site.

I only discovered about using WordPress as an online store when I was about to ditch Volusion for good. Like most people, I only knew that you could either sell on eBay or your own online store. For the most part, beginner sellers will use eBay to get started. They assume that you need a huge budget to create an online store. So, they never consider having an online store when they start selling online.

My first venture into the online retails

For some people, selling items which were lying in their house was their starting point. That was how I got started with selling physical products online. I began with selling my used magazines online. I admitted that it was a nerve wrecking when I started my so-called selling career. I wondered if anyone would buy my magazines. But at the same time, I didn't have much expectation since I wouldn't lose money if I couldn't sell any of them.

A week after I began selling on eBay, I started to get a few customers who wanted to buy my magazines. It was fun to make money selling whatever stuff I had lying around in my house, but selling on eBay comes with a caveat. Listing your items on eBay weren't free. You had to pay for it. And what was the worst part? It might not guarantee that people would see your listing. It was a different story if you had an eBay store.

A few weeks after selling online on eBay, I signed up for eBay store. Was it worth investing? Unfortunately, it wasn't worth it at all. The only perks you had were being able to list down more items than the standard account. And the listing fees were still applicable even if you had an eBay store. So, it was a rash decision on my side to sign up for eBay store. What can I say? I was naïve about business at that time.

But still, I couldn't care less about it since the only thing I cared was for the items to sell. While eBay seemed to be the fastest way for you to get your items sold, eBay had too many rules that didn't make sense to me. My memory about selling on eBay was vague to me since it was a long time ago. At that time, eBay allowed me to list up to 60 items for free. But for some weird reason, they began to pester me to pay when I listed my eleventh item.

Not only that, eBay forced me to charge $5 at most for the cheapest shipping option for shipping within the US. Well, that was the rule for eBay US. It made sense to charge at most $5 for a shipping rate if I lived in the US. But I was an international seller. The cheapest shipping I could charge for the shipping with tracking was around $6 to $7. Since I couldn't offer $5 for registered airmail, I could only ship the items using SAL.

Seeing that I had so many restrictions selling on eBay, I've decided to start my own online store for a change. And that was the time I discovered ProStores. The ironic part was it was an e-commerce solution by the same company that brought eBay to life. Without much thought, I've decided to sign up for ProStores. And I began to export my eBay listing to my brand new ProStores account to get started.

Sure, it might seem too much for someone like me to setup an online store to sell used items. But for some reason, I didn't do it to sell the used items. At that time, I already made up my mind to do a different kind of business. And that was selling Asian women clothing brands. To be honest, I had no idea what was I thinking back then. I didn't have much experience with the retail business, other than selling used items on eBay. But I did it.

I didn't remember how long it took me to finish everything. But it took me around two weeks to take things off the ground. I only signed up for the basic tier which was enough for me. Thus, my career as the owner of online fashion retail began. I was lucky that I could handle all the technical stuff of the business. At least I had something that I could do on my own.

While I was happy to make a transition to ProStores, I did notice that ProStores lacked many things. Because of that, I had to rely on many third party apps to compensate ProStores' lack of features. Some of the apps were free. But it was still a hassle. An e-commerce solution like ProStores should have everything that online sellers needed.

Now, what ProStores lacks, you ask? One of the things that ProStores didn't have was a mobile-optimized website. Sure, a mobile-optimized website wasn't a trend back then. But I knew that some of us were browsing an online store on their mobile phone during the break or when they were bored. So, having a mobile-optimized website would put my business way above everyone else. After all, only a few websites were mobile-optimized back then.

I was proud of the fact that I was way ahead than everyone else in the business. But ProStores didn't. If I wanted to have a mobile-optimized website, then I had to hire a developer to do it for me. I was the sort of person who preferred bootstrapping over anything else. So, hiring a developer was not an option for me.

And that led me to another problem with ProStores. I had no idea what these people at ProStores thought when they coded ProStores. They didn't use the common web coding language like HTML and CSS. Instead, they created a brand new coding language for ProStores called SSML. On the surface, it looked like your usual HTML and CSS. The only difference was it had different syntax. Luckily, they did provide a dedicated document about SSML. It was for those who were interested to find out more about the coding.

What got me to play around with SSML code of my site was because I had to customize the theme. WordPress premium theme was still affordable enough for bootstrapping businesses. But the premium website templates for ProStores were beyond affordable to me. You had to spend hundreds of dollars only to get the premium template. I had no idea how much it would cost me to hire a designer to come up with a web design for my store.

And what's even worst, you couldn't just hire anyone to do the job. You needed to hire someone who knew ProStores. And it was too bad that only a few people knew about its existence. So, you could only hire a designer who was ProStores certified. You could get a list from ProStores website itself, though. But expect to pay a premium price even for something minor.

Could you just hire Bill, a web developer who lived next door? Sure, you could do that. But be sure to give him the SSML document. Somehow, he might charge you the same as the ProStores certified designers and developers. It wasn't a standard coding. And it was hell to understand.

But if you were like me who rather took things to your own hand, then their complete guide about SSML was handy too. It was a bit overwhelming at first. But I was glad that I managed to handle it well enough without messing the look of my website. It wasn't a bright idea to attempt something technical on my own. But knowing the technical side of things was beneficial in my business. And I still hold that belief even until today.

If you didn't feel like messing around with the code, then you could use the available free themes right off the bat. But the free themes that they provided were so ugly. It looked more like the designs were for the website in the 80s. I love anything vintage or vintage-inspired fashion style. But vintage look doesn't do any justice when it comes to web design. Since I hated the web design, I just had to play around with SSML code. At least it looked much better than the original one after a few minor modifications.

Despite its lacking critical features, I still stuck to ProStores for two years. So, why I was still sticking to ProStores? Well, it was the only e-commerce I knew that used PayPal for the monthly billing. Well, ProStores was under eBay. And PayPal was the only option for me to pay the monthly billing.

A few years after I moved out of ProStores, I received an email from them. It was about eBay's decision to close down ProStores. They also urged all businesses to migrate to other e-commerce solutions. Like most businesses, I found it hard to believe that they've decided to close down ProStores. But I guess it was the best decision for them. After all, ProStores lacked so many features that were common in many e-commerce solutions. And they were far behind compared to other e-commerce solutions out there.

Starting a business with a brand new e-commerce solution

It was funny that I refused to make a switch despite ProStores' lack of features. And I still didn't switch to another platform even after they increased the price for all tiers. It was a hassle to me since I had to move hundreds of listing from ProStores to another e-commerce solution. Like any other migration, it cost money for moving data to another platform.

At that time, I came across a few popular e-commerce solutions. Some of them were Volusion, Big Commerce, and Shopify. Unlike the last time, I made a careful consideration on which e-commerce solution I had to use. I didn't like the idea of spending time with migrating data to a new site. So, I had to be sure that it was an e-commerce solution that I loved and beneficial to my business.

After looking through many different options, I settled down with Volusion. Budget-wise, Volusion was a lot pricier than my current tier on ProStores. But it did have everything that I needed for my online store. It was a lot more superior to ProStores in every single way. So, I signed up with a similar tier that I had in ProStores and began my migration to Volusion.

Once my brand new online store was open, I felt

that migrating to Volusion was the best decision I've ever made. Everything felt amazing until one day, my billing for that month exceeded the amount that I had to pay. It was devastating that my expenses for that month were more than the expenditure for the previous month.

It seemed that I exceeded my bandwidth for that month. And the exceeded bandwidth had nothing to do with the increased traffic to my online store. The reason for the exceeded bandwidth was because I kept logging in to the admin panel. Unlike ProStores, I had to login into my admin panel via my storefront. As a result, it looked more like there was a lot of incoming traffic even though it was me who was logging in on a daily basis.

I did explain the situation to the customer support. What they suggested me to do was to turn off CDN. CDN stands for Content Delivery Network. With CDN, it will replicate your website on a different server across the globe. It will make your website load faster since it will load based on where your visitor is located. Turning off CDN would mean that my online store would be much slower for visitors outside of the US.

At this point, I felt that the same thing would occur to me again in my next billing cycle. So, I've decided to find another solution. I wanted it to be more cost-effective, easier to manage and wouldn't exceed my bandwidth. Even if it would exceed the bandwidth, it had a lot to do with a massive traffic to my website which didn't cause by me.

I hate to say this, but it seemed like I had to migrate to another platform again. At that point, I could only hope that it would be my last time migrating to another platform.

My encounter with WordPress e-commerce
Before I had a problem with Volusion, I was playing around with WooCommerce. The plugin itself was free, but they also provided a demo for you to test run the plugin. I signed up for the demo because I was curious. I never thought that my encounter with WooCommerce became my turning point.

After thinking through, I made up my mind to switch to WordPress. It wasn't that hard for me to figure out about WordPress. I had a self-hosted WordPress site before, so I was already familiar with it before I made the switch. And what was the best part? I still had the same feature that I had when I was still using Volusion. It was possible thanks to WordPress plugins.

As usual, the migration wasn't easy. But I didn't

mind as long as I no longer had to rely on Volusion. I had to work long hours to migrate everything to WordPress before my next billing cycle. I notified the customer support a few weeks later that I no longer wanted to use Volusion anymore.

Moving to WordPress was indeed the best decision I've ever made. My monthly bill was less than what I paid when I was still using Volusion. You have no idea how amazing it is when your expenses became a lot lower than before.

You don't have to undergo the same experience as I do
So, why am I telling you this story? Well, it's simple. I want to let you know that I didn't know any better when I started selling online. In fact, I was struggling to set up a WordPress site. I thought that buying a domain name on WordPress.com was the same as having a self-hosted WordPress site.

I didn't know that those were two different things. There are many tutorials on how to setup a self-hosted WordPress site on YouTube. But only a few tutorials focus specifically on using WordPress to create an online store. Okay, turning a WordPress site into a full-fledged e-commerce site isn't that hard. That is if you're already familiar with WordPress. But I wish that somebody would tell me about it. At least I didn't have to spend hours only to find the best solution for my business.

Besides the technical side, you also have to figure out the management side of the business too. I doubt that the web developers can help you with this part since they don't know any better. It's a different story if they also own an online store. That is if you know a web developer who is generous enough to give a tip or two to you.

I don't mean to toot my own horn, but what I'm going to share with you in this book will be much different than you expect. In this book, I'm going to tell you everything I know about creating an online store and manage it like a pro. So, you can expect what I say in this book is based on my experience. I'm writing this book as a business owner, not as a web developer. And not even as a business consultant. I wish that I had a book like this so then I can avoid making mistakes that cost me a lot of money.

Don't worry if you feel overwhelmed with the idea of creating and managing your online store on your own. Based on my story alone, it's clear how clueless I was back then. And I made a lot of mistakes that caused me to lose sales along the way too. At least I was fortunate that I didn't receive hate mails from the angry customers. Put that into the mix, I bet that it's going to be a wild ride.

It's sad that I had to close down Fashion Paraizo after being around in business for almost five years. I was no longer passionate about what I did. So, it was an obvious decision for me to close it down since it no longer served me. With Fashion Paraizo was no longer active, I decided to turn it into a sample store instead. You can take a look at the sample store yourself if you'd like to see how an online store on WordPress looks like.

Now, let's take a look at why I encourage people to use WordPress to create an online store instead.

CHAPTER 2

Why WordPress?

I love WordPress for many reasons. So, I will always recommend people to use the self-hosted WordPress for any website they want to create. It can be a bit intimidating for beginners. But WordPress is the most flexible content management solution (CMS) I've ever used. And that explains why all my websites are on WordPress.

Besides its flexibility, WordPress is free too. But you have to pay for other things such as hosting and a domain name. You can also get premium WordPress theme and premium WordPress plugins too. Keep in mind that I'm not talking about WordPress.com here. WordPress.com and the self-hosted WordPress are two different things. If you want to create an online store, you need to use the self-hosted WordPress, not WordPress.com.

Assuming that you're not as picky as me, then the only thing you have to pay is the hosting and the domain name. The good news is it won't cost you a lot of money. So, it won't cause a hole in your pocket even if your business hasn't yet picked up the momentum. Keep in mind that the business cost will increase as your business grows.

With so many good things about WordPress, here are more reasons for you to consider. Note that the comparison is between WordPress and e-commerce solutions.

1. WordPress premium theme is cheaper than the premium themes for the e-commerce solution

Remember my experience with ProStores? If you're using an e-commerce solution such as Volusion, you have to shell out a lot of money only for a web template. These web templates come with a hefty price tag. And it doesn't include the price you have to pay if you want them to customize the look that caters to your brand.

E-commerce solution like Big Commerce provides a professional-looking theme for all tiers. And they're available for free. As for other e-commerce solutions, you have to pay for it. And I doubt that the templates are user-friendly for a novice. In the end, you have to hire a designer if you want to do a slight tweaking on the template.

Premium WordPress themes usually cost around $100 and below. And what I love about these WordPress themes is it's flexible enough to customize on your own. Premium WordPress themes come with a framework and a child theme. If you make a modification on your child theme, it will only alter the design of your website. It won't affect other functionalities of your site thanks to the framework.

Some premium WordPress themes also offer annual membership. So, the cost for the premium theme will be much lower. One of them is Elegant Themes, where the membership will cost $69 per year and $250 for a one-time fee. Regardless of what tier you choose, it will include other WordPress themes they have. If you only want to buy only one premium theme, there are many places to buy besides Elegant Themes.

What's even better, you can use the same theme on your other website or someone else's website. Be sure to check the developer's terms and conditions about using the same theme on another site. For the most part, they allow you to use the same theme on a different website, whether you own the website or not.

2. There are many plugins (free and paid) that can help your online store

What differentiates one WordPress site to another isn't only the WordPress theme. The plugins that you use can also differentiate the look and feel of your WordPress site. Different plugins will give you a different functionality for your WordPress site. But some premium WordPress themes already include the basic features in the framework. So, you don't need to install a lot of plugins to get the customized look.

There are many plugins to choose from, whether they're free or paid. Even for the paid plugins, it still won't cost you a lot of money. Not only that, but you can also use the same premium plugins on different sites, as long as you own the website. You need to look for the multi-site license if you decided to use the same plugin on other sites that you own.

3. There is no limitation on how many products you can list and the bandwidth

Remember my bandwidth issue with Volusion? With WordPress, you don't have to worry so much about the bandwidth, at least in the beginning of your business. Hosting like Hostgator has an unlimited bandwidth for the shared hosting plan. That's the basic hosting plan, which is good enough for starters.

Of course, you will exceed your bandwidth when you have so many visitors coming to your online store. In this scenario, you can upgrade to WordPress hosting plan. It can cater for the high volume of traffic coming to your website.

4. You can have a blog and run it side-by-side with your online store

WordPress also allows you to have a blog and have it running together with your online store. You can choose to create a blog section under the same domain or create a subdomain for the blog.

5. Virtual assistants are most likely to be familiar with WordPress

If you're thinking of hiring people for your online store, it won't be a problem for you. Most freelance web developers and designers are already familiar with WordPress. After all, it's a widely known platform, and many businesses are using WordPress. You can find many people who can create a new theme and develop the plugins for you. They can also do the website maintenance for you as well.

Chapter Recap

You can create any website with WordPress. And that includes creating an online store. The reason why I recommend WordPress is because it's cost-effective. And many developers are already familiar with it. What's even better, WordPress is perfect for a novice and also for the nontech-savvy as well.

CHAPTER 3

Registering Your Domain Name

My first experience with buying my own domain name was when I bought it for my WordPress blog. At that time, I made a mistake by buying a domain name at WordPress.com. I thought that it was a self-hosted WordPress site. It turned out to be that wasn't the case at all. Even if you have a domain name for your site, your site is still hosted on WordPress.com.

And it doesn't have the same customization as the self-hosted WordPress site.

Okay, how come I make a mistake like this one? Well, it was easy to buy a domain name in ProStores or any e-commerce solution for that matter. But I failed to realize that a self-hosted WordPress site doesn't only need its own domain name. I also need to have a hosting plan as well.

And that explains why it's called self-hosted WordPress site. You own that domain name and a hosting for your WordPress site since you pay for it. Because of my costly mistake, I ended up spending $15 for a domain name which I could get cheaper elsewhere. After almost a year, I transferred that domain name to another domain registrar. It's a fancy name for a website that sells a domain name.

If you plan to have a self-hosted WordPress site, you need to have a domain name. Same goes with the online stores created using an e-commerce solution. Buying a domain name can be a click away in most e-commerce solutions. But that's not the case for the self-hosted WordPress sites. You have to get it from a domain registrar. The price for the domain name varies, depending on which domain registrar that you buy from.

Choosing your domain name

Before you run off to get a domain name for your online store, it's important to note that your domain name is your brand. You need to think hard about naming your online store. Once you already buy the domain name, you can no longer change it. It's a different story if you plan to let the domain name expires after one year and buy a new one for your online store.

Your domain name shouldn't only reflect your brand. But it also should be something that's easy to spell. It's fine for you to come up with a unique name. But be sure it's something that can be spelled by a normal human being. You don't want people to end up on the wrong site only because they misspell your online store's name.

Another thing to note is the use of symbol and numbers in your domain name. For example, if your domain name is 2livelife.com, people might type to or two instead of the number 2. It's because that's what they heard when you introduced your online store. And it can be very confusing to your customers. So, it would be best for you to stick with words instead. The usage of dash (-) may not be a good idea too because people might assume that your domain name is free from the dash.

If I can start all over again, I would have named my online store with something catchy, modern and hip. The name Fashion Paraizo seemed like a blah name to me. The catchy but easy-to-spell name isn't just memorable to your customers. But it also represents your brand. When people mention your store name, they already expect what sort of things you sell. It also helps with bringing the right customers to your online store.

Where to buy the domain name
There are many places to choose from when it comes to buying a domain name. And these places also sell other things too such as SSL Certificates and WhoisGuard. You need SSL Certificate to accept credit card payment. And you need WhoisGuard to protect your domain name from the prying eyes. They can be spammers, marketing firms, and online fraudsters.

Most domain registrars will encourage you to buy WhoisGuard when you buy a new domain name. Same goes with transferring an existing domain from another registrar. It only costs you $2.88 per year. Your domain registrar will notify you when your WhoisGuard subscription expired. At the same time, they will also send a reminder to renew your domain ownership as well.

Here are some of the places that you can buy a domain name from. The price varies depending on what kind of domain extension you buy.

1. Namecheap

Namecheap is a place where I buy all my domain names from. I love to buy from Namecheap because the domain name here is a lot cheaper than other domain registrars. Their domain name costs $12.88 per year for .COM extension. They also have a special promotion for new domain names from time to time too. Some of the promotions need you to have a coupon code for the special offer. But you can always find the coupon code on their blog.

2. GoDaddy

GoDaddy is also another place that people love to get their domain names from. The domain name here is pricier than Namecheap, where it costs $15.17 per year for .COM extension. But their domain name is a lot cheaper when you get it when they're having a promotion. But the discounted rate is only applicable for the first year only. You still have to pay a normal price when you renew your domain name.

3. 1&1

What I love about 1&1 is that you can register a .COM domain name for only $0.99. But keep in mind that it's only applicable for the first year. And the offer is only available for certain countries only. You should expect to pay $14.99 per year whenever you renew your domain name here.

4. Enom

I didn't know that all domain names from ProStores are from Enom. I only knew about it when I asked ProStores' customer support. At that time I wanted to transfer Fashion Paraizo domain name to Namecheap. I could choose to stick with Enom if I wanted to, but I didn't have direct access to manage the domain name on Enom. So, it was unfortunate that I have no idea how good Enom is as a domain registrar.

Many well-known sites such as Symantec and The Seattle Times are using Enom as their domain registrar. Enom is cheaper than GoDaddy. But it still not as cheap as Namecheap, where a domain name with .COM extension costs you $13.95 per year.

5. iWantMyName

What I love about iWantMyName is it has a one-click process for domain mapping. But it's a shame that the one-click domain mapping process is only for platforms like Shopify and Tumblr. I got a domain name for my Tumblr blog from iWantMyName before. It's unfortunate that they don't have a one-click domain mapping process for WordPress. So, you still have to do a manual domain mapping if you buy a domain name from iWantMyName.

This domain registrar is perfect if you need a domain name for your Shopify store or Tumblr blog. After all, you don't need to mess around with your domain setting. All you need to do is to install Shopify apps in your domain and do a slight configuration on your Shopify account. It will do the mapping process automatically after that. The price for the domain name with .COM extension is $14.90 per year.

Domain name extension

You can find many types of domain name extension in all domain registrars. You can choose to buy the usual .COM extension or the unique extensions like .IO, .SHOP and much more. Getting a unique domain extension is perfect for differentiating yourself from the competitors. But keep in mind that the unique extensions like those don't come cheap. It will only become cheap during the first year of your domain ownership. They will charge you the regular price during your second term.

Not to mention, the price for the unique extension is the same regardless of where you buy them. I admit that the .COM extension may seem blah to you. But then again, it's still the best option for your online store if you stick to using .COM extension. After all, most people are so accustomed to a domain name which ends with .COM. They may not be used to the unique extensions. That is unless your target audience is a tech-savvy people. And you're only targeting people from a specific country.

Some domain names are not available for sale if somebody else already buys the domain name. If the domain name that you want is not available for the .COM extension, then you have to come up with another name. You can also try to find the same name with a different extension. If it's still the same, then I guess it doesn't hurt for you to get that unique domain extension for your online store. Maybe your online store name is meant to have a unique domain extension from the beginning.

Chapter Recap

Before you can get your online store up and running, you need to get a domain name for your online store. Think of it like registering an online store name for your business. Once you already secure the domain name, the name will belong to you. Keep in mind that you need to renew the domain name on a yearly basis. If you don't, your domain name will expire. And someone else will be able to claim the same domain name that you used before.

CHAPTER 4

Getting a Hosting Plan for Your Online Store

If you want to create your own website, you need to have a server to host your website. Getting a server for your site is not cheap. And there are other things you need to consider such as the security of your server. If you're not careful, someone else will be able to hack into your server. You can lose everything if the hacker gets a hold of your server.

The good news is you don't have to get yourself a server if you want to create your own website. Same goes for creating an online store. That's when getting a hosting plan for your website makes sense. It's not only from the technical aspect, but also from the financial perspective as well. The cost of getting a hosting plan is much cheaper than getting a server. And it also saves you tons of headaches from the technical side of maintaining your server.

There are many types of hosting plan to choose from. And it can be daunting if it's your first time purchasing a hosting plan, especially if you don't know anything about it. This chapter will explain what sort of hosting plan you should get for your online store. And when do you need a more expensive hosting plan for your online store.

The type of server available

There are many varieties when it comes to hosting plan. But in general, it will boil down to three different types. And they're shared hosting, VPS hosting and dedicated hosting. Shared hosting simply means that you'll be sharing the same server with other people. So, you will have a specific amount of space and bandwidth. Shared hosting is perfect for the new website owner. It's cheap, and it's ideal for sites that don't have a large volume of traffic.

Dedicated hosting is like what the name implied. It only means that the server will have your website only. Since you own the whole server to yourself, it will cost a lot more than the shared hosting plan. You may need a dedicated hosting plan if you have such a large website like Amazon. And you have a high volume of traffic coming to your site.

If dedicated hosting is expensive to you, then you can opt for VPS hosting. It has more or less the same capabilities as the dedicated hosting. But it has less technical specification than the dedicated hosting. So, VPS hosting is perfect if your website starts to grow in the audience. And it needs a higher server complexity.

All types of servers are perfect for any WordPress sites. But if you only plan to host WordPress sites, there's also a dedicated hosting for WordPress sites only. Like VPS hosting and dedicated hosting, it's also for websites that have a high volume of traffic.

What to look for in a hosting plan
For WordPress sites, it's best to look for a hosting plan that provides a one-click installation. With one-

click installation, it allows you to install WordPress on your server easily. The only thing you need to do is to configure settings like the admin name and password. Once you already complete the configuration, you need to wait for a moment for your brand new website to go live.

Before you can install WordPress on your server, you need to locate the name server. You need the name server to do the domain mapping. You can begin the process after you buy the domain name from your domain registrar. It's not that hard to find the name server for your hosting. In hosting like Hostgator, you can find it in the sidebar of your CPanel. I admit that it may sound technical to you. But don't worry. It's not difficult as it seems.

There are many places that you can get your hosting plan from. And they're also widely recommended by many business owners and web developers.

1. Hostgator

When it comes to hosting, my personal favorite is Hostgator. It's the same hosting I use to host my site. Not only Hostgator has one-click installation feature. But you can choose to pay the hosting either annually or monthly. You will save a lot more if you choose to pay the bill annually. Not only that, but you can also opt to pay either using a credit card or PayPal.

Hostgator offers three different types of shared plan. Their hatchling plan is for hosting one website. And their Baby Plan allows you to host many different websites. Their Business Plan is the only plan that includes a private SSL. It's a short name for security socket layer. You need SSL to process confidential data. It can be personal details and credit card information. Their Business Plan also includes free toll number. It's perfect for businesses who are taking a phone order.

2. Bluehost

Many people that I know are using Bluehost when they get started. From the technical perspective, Bluehost isn't that much different from Hostgator. But their hosting plan includes a free domain. They also have a dedicated hosting for the online store. It's called WooCommerce hosting. The hosting plan is the same as Hostgator Business Plan.

Since Bluehost provides a free domain, it can be a heaven sent to you. Well, you don't have to buy a domain name separately. And you can manage both your domain name and hosting in one place. While it may seem convenient to you, it's not a good idea to have a domain name and hosting at the same place. It's for the security reason. If someone hacks into your website, they get not only a hold of your server, but also your domain name too.

Once they change the ownership of the domain, it'll be hard for you to get it back. And that's the reason why it's not a wise thing to have your domain name and the hosting under the same account. Now it makes sense why you need to have a domain name separated from your hosting account.

One of the drawbacks about Bluehost is they only have annual billing and no monthly billing. So, Bluehost is not an option for you if you don't have the budget to pay the hosting annually. But if you want to save a lot more on the annual billing, then Bluehost is the best option for you. Their price is much lower than Hostgator when it comes to the annual billing.

Both Hostgator and Bluehost offer the migration process to their server. You need to pay $149.99 if you want a seamless migration to Bluehost. But Hostgator provides free transfers to the new account within 30 days of sign-up.

3. Media Temple

Media Temple offers similar hosting types like Hostgator and Bluehost. Unlike Hostgator and

Bluehost, Media Temple's Personal Hosting Plan can host up to 100 sites. If you're planning to host tons of niche websites, then Media Temple is worth it. But if you only want to host 2 or 3 websites, it may not be worth paying since their basic tier costs $20 per month.

4. SiteGround
SiteGround also offers similar hosting types like Hostgator, Bluehost and Media Temple. But what makes them stand out more is because of their WordPress hosting plans. It's a shame that their WordPress hosting plan isn't for the website with a high volume of traffic. Their WordPress hosting plan is the same like Hostgator Shared Hosting Plan. But it's more specific for WordPress sites.

You still need to get Hostgator WordPress Cloud Hosting if you have a high volume of traffic. You can also give WPEngine a try since it's also a hosting for high volume WordPress sites.

Brief intro about WordPress hosting
Both Hostgator and Bluehost also offer WordPress hosting. As the name implied, it's a specific hosting plan for WordPress sites only. You can choose to get WordPress hosting if you have a budget to do so.

After all, WordPress hosting costs more than the shared hosting plan.

So, when is the perfect time for you to switch to WordPress hosting? You can switch to WordPress hosting if you have a high volume of traffic coming to your website. And you already exceed the bandwidth allocation in your shared hosting plan. WordPress hosting has similar capabilities as a dedicated hosting. But it costs less since WordPress hosting hosts WordPress sites only.

There are many places that you can get WordPress hosting from. A few of them are Hostgator and Bluehost. But Hostgator WordPress Cloud Hosting is the cheapest among them. That is when you compare it with other hosting like WPEngine and Media Temple.

Price-wise, Hostgator is a clear winner. But then again, who should use WPEngine and Media Temple? Let's take a look at what both WPEngine and Media Temple has to offer.

1. WPEngine

WPEngine costs more if you're only hosting one website. But it's cheaper if you plan to host up to 150 WordPress sites that receive a high volume of traffic every month. So, WPEngine is perfect if you're a web developer. And your clients' websites have a significant amount of traffic coming to their site. But if you only create a website for yourself, you couldn't care less about what WPEngine has to offer.

But what if you have more than one website that gets a high volume of traffic every month? Then Hostgator WordPress Cloud Hosting is the best option for you. They not only have a plan for one website, but they also have a plan for two websites and five websites. Despite what plans you choose, it still costs less than the plans in WPEngine.

2. Media Temple

Media Temple also has more or less similar target market like WPEngine. But price-wise, Media Temple is cheaper than WPEngine. This comparison is based on Media Temple's Personal Plan and WPEngine's Personal Plan. Media Temple's Personal Plan only costs $20 per month and allows two websites. WPEngine's Personal Plan costs $29 per month and allows one website only.

The good news doesn't end here

Hosting like Hostgator and Bluehost will always have a special offer from time to time. If you want a deep discount for your chosen plan, then be sure to follow me on Twitter for Hostgator and Bluehost promotion. They usually don't advertise these special offers on their website. So, you can only get your hand on these offers on my Twitter account.

But if you don't feel like waiting to get the best deal for your hosting plan, you can use my Hostgator's exclusive coupon code, EFFICIENT to receive 25% off on any hosting plan in the first month. All you need to do is to add the coupon code during the checkout process to receive the discount.

Chapter Recap
Besides a domain name, you need a hosting plan to host your online store. A shared hosting plan is perfect for new business. But you need to be sure that your hosting plan has a dedicated IP address for hosting SSL certificate. You'll find out more about SSL certificate in the later chapter.

CHAPTER 5

Turning Your WordPress Site into an Online Store

I mentioned before that WordPress is originally used for blogging. With a little bit of customization, you can turn any WordPress sites into anything you desire. Want to create a membership site besides creating a typical WordPress site and a blog? All you need to do is to install a membership site plugin and customize it in any way you want.

Thanks to plugins, you can have many different features running at the same time. You can take the same concept with running an online store on your WordPress. You can have an online store component and have a blog running at the same time. You can also create a special pricing for the wholesalers and registered members as well.

There are many e-commerce plugins for WordPress to choose from. Some of the e-commerce plugins will turn your WordPress site into an online store. And there are also a few plugins that work as a shopping cart plugin. This kind of plugin will redirect you to the shopping cart plugin website. From there, your customers can choose to pay either credit card or PayPal.

These e-commerce plugins may seem like an all-rounder to you and me. But that's not the case if we take a look at these plugins in greater details. So, the type of plugins you choose will depend on what sort of online store you like to create.

E-commerce plugins that will turn your WordPress site into a complete online store

These e-commerce plugins will turn your whole WordPress site into an online store. This plugin also gives you the same feature like the e-commerce solution. Install an e-commerce plugin if you want to turn your WordPress site into an online store.

You can install the plugins directly from WordPress plugin directory. Same goes with the premium e-commerce plugins that offer the lite version of the plugins. Be sure that you already registered and received a license key before you can activate the plugin.

Here are some of the plugins that can turn your WordPress site into an online store. Different plugins will have different features, depending on your needs.

1. WP eCommerce

According to WP eCommerce website, it's the original e-commerce plugin. I have no idea about that since I was late into the game when I discovered about it. Because of that, many plugins are built specifically for WP eCommerce. Not only that, there are many premium themes available for WP eCommerce as well. WP eCommerce was the first plugin I used on Fashion Paraizo when I moved my online store to WordPress.

The setting for this e-commerce plugin is not that difficult. But I hate the fact that the plugin crashes the whole website whenever I update the plugin. Okay, it was my fault that I didn't have a backup for my site. But I didn't know that the update was severe enough to crash the whole site. I'm not sure whether the new version is no longer causing the problem. But I won't recommend anyone to use this plugin regardless of what WP eCommerce claims.

Putting my nasty experience aside, this plugin allows me to add an extra field on the checkout page. On the checkout page, I ask them how they find out about my store. This extra information allows me to know what marketing channel I need to focus more on. Another field that I add is what I should do if the items that they order are no longer available. This information will help me to do what's best for my customers since all items I sell are pre-order items.

The plugin is available for free and premium version. The premium version offers more payment gateways, technical support, and shipping option.

2. WooCommerce

WooCommerce is another e-commerce plugin for WordPress. I began to use this plugin after my nasty experience with WP eCommerce. Back then, you can give this plugin a try on their website before you install it on your server. All you have to do is to sign up for the demo, and they will give you a password to access the demo on their website.

During the testing, I realized that I couldn't add the extra fields in the checkout page. Not only that, the shipping configuration was too basic. You need to use a premium extension if you want to offer more shipping options for your customers. Luckily, the current version of WooCommerce has an improved shipping configuration. So, you don't need to use the premium extension for more shipping options.

Unlike WP eCommerce, WooCommerce is a lot more stable. I didn't experience any of the crashing issues whenever I update the plugin. But then again, it's still better for you to have a backup for your online store. What's even better, the plugin is completely free. And they have more extensions compared to WP eCommerce.

I highly recommend this plugin because not only it is free. But it also gives you similar features like an e-commerce solution. It's the same plugin I use in the sample store, in case you're wondering. On top of that, there are many premium WordPress themes that are compatible with this plugin. And there are also many apps that support a direct integration with WooCommerce as well.

3. MarketPress

MarketPress is another plugin you can use besides WP eCommerce and WooCommerce. Unlike WP eCommerce and WooCommerce, MarketPress has everything you need in one plugin. So, you don't have to depend on the extensions to get the features that you need. But you can still use other extensions if you feel that the available features are still not enough for you.

The only downside is you can only access this plugin if you join WPMU DEV subscription for only $49 per month. But they also offer a free 14-day trial if you're interested in giving MarketPress a try. Besides MarketPress plugin, you will also get other premium WordPress plugins and themes. They also provide WordPress support and WordPress training course as well.

4. Jigoshop

Jigoshop is an e-commerce plugin like WooCommerce. Just like WooCommerce, they also provide extensions and themes specifically for Jigoshop. What I love about Jigoshop is their premium extensions are a one-time fee. But in WooCommerce, you have to pay annually for the continuous support and usage for the plugins.

5. Cart66

Cart 66 is another premium e-commerce plugin for WordPress. Unlike MarketPress, Cart66 only costs $9.99 per month or $99 per year, with two months free. If you want extra features, you can choose to opt for their Fire Plan. The plan costs $29.99 per month or $299 per year, with two months free.

What I love about Cart 66 is you don't need to have SSL certificate thanks to its feature, Cart66 Cloud. Cart66 Cloud uses subdomains to make your checkout page much secure. It works the same like having SSL certificate on your online store. Another thing I love about Cart66 is you can use it with all WordPress themes.

You can try Cart66 free for 14 days to see it for yourself. Once your trial period is over, you can choose which payment plan that suits your preference.

Shopping cart plugins

Unlike e-commerce plugins, shopping cart plugins are easier to set up. And it won't turn your site into a complete online store. If your WordPress site is a blog, it will remain the same. After installing the shopping cart plugin, you only need to configure the plugin. And you can start selling right away after that. It doesn't even add extra pages such as a checkout page and order detail page.

The customers then will complete the payment at the plugins' secured website. Your customers' detail will be available in that shopping cart website. And you will fulfill your order there. You can also access your sales report in the dashboard as well. Of course, you have to sign up with them first and upload your products there. You will get a specific link for the product after that. You can use the link to post it on your site or promote it on your social media account.

Since the process is rather simple, you don't have to mess around with the settings. And it takes less time to configure the plugin too. A platform like this is also perfect if you don't have a website. After all, each item will have a specific link after you upload it to the shopping cart site itself. And you can use the links to drive traffic to the products directly with social media or your blog.

Not all shopping cart plugins will redirect your customers to complete the sale. You can make this plugin processes the orders without having your customers to leave your site. To do that, you need to get SSL certificate for your site. You should consult with the shopping cart plugin you use on the type of SSL certificate you should get. After all, different SSL certificates have a different level of validation.

Shopping cart plugins are perfect if you only sell a handful of physical items. But it can be impractical if you have a lot of items to sell. So, I don't recommend any retailers to use shopping cart plugins. That is unless they only plan to sell a few items on their website. But there are some shopping cart plugins that will give you a shortcode for your listing. You can then add the shortcode anywhere on your site, making the process seamless on your side.

I use the shopping cart plugin to sell my e-books because of how convenient it is. And I don't need to have full e-commerce features only to sell e-books on my website. Here are some of the shopping cart plugins that you can use on your site. Some plugins not only allow you to sell physical and digital products. But you can also sell subscriptions and memberships as well.

1. Gumroad

Gumroad allows you to sell both physical and digital products on your site. Gumroad is what I'm using on my website, The Efficient You and also on my fiction author site, Sekina Mayu. It's easy to get started with selling on Gumroad. All you need to do is to upload the products there. And you can use the product links to post on your site or your social media accounts.

Gumroad also offers your customers to pay either using a credit card or PayPal. So, you don't even need to have a merchant account and a payment gateway for taking the credit card payment. Gumroad only takes a certain percentage of fees from your total sales. If you use the free version of Gumroad, the fee is only 8.5% + 30 cents per transaction. The premium version only costs you $10 per month where the fee is 3.5% + 30 cents per sale.

Once you've accumulated at least $10 in your Gumroad account, they will send you the payment every Friday. You can accept your payment with PayPal for international sellers. They also offer payment through Direct Deposit for those who live in the USA, Canada, the UK and Australia. This option may seem okay with people who are selling digital products. But it can be tough if you're selling physical products. Some of you may want immediate access to your fund to cover the shipping fees.

Not only that, but they also have Gumroad Discover. It's a place where you can discover other people who are also selling on Gumroad. Think of this feature like the better version of eBay marketplace. They only take extra 10% fees for the sales generated from Gumroad Discover. I can't be so sure how effective it is since I never have any sales coming from there. You can disable your products from appearing in Gumroad Discover if you want.

Another reason why I love to use Gumroad is that they have affiliate features. If you want to boost your sales with the help of affiliate marketers, then you can use this feature on Gumroad. But they need to have an account on Gumroad first before they can become your affiliate. I've yet to try this feature. But it's a bonus if you want to boost your sales with affiliate marketing that won't be a hassle on your side.

Gumroad is perfect if you're selling a few physical products and digital products. But for selling physical products, be sure that you have enough budgets to cover the shipping cost. The last thing you want is your customers are complaining that you take a long time to fulfill their orders. It's a different story if you tell them that you will only process all orders on Friday.

2. Selz

Selz has similar features like Gumroad. But you can create your own professional webstore and have your own custom domain with Selz. In a nutshell,

Selz can be a cross between Gumroad and an e-commerce solution like Shopify. If you prefer to feature your products on your WordPress site, you can do so. But if you don't, you can create an online store straight from Selz without ever needing a WordPress site.

There are different plans to choose from. So, it depends on what sort of features you need for your online store. Plans start from $12.99 per month, but they also have a free plan, which allows you to sell up to 5 items. They also offer a free trial for the first 14 days if you'd like to give Selz a try. Regardless of your plan, you still have to pay 2% for the transaction fee and 2.9% + 30 cents for the processing fee per sales.

If you want something like Shopify but cheaper, then consider signing up with Selz. I've tried Selz in the past when I was offering a freelance work. But now, I'm using Gumroad since I no longer offer freelance work anymore. And I'm currently selling digital products on my website.

3. Shopify Buy Button

Shopify Buy Button is another option besides Gumroad and Selz. It has the same feature like the one you can get from Shopify Store. You can also add the apps from Shopify app store if you want more features for your online store. The plan starts at $9 per month, with free 14 day trials if you'd like to give Shopify Buy Button a try.

Personally, I don't recommend you to use Shopify Buy Button. That is unless you already have an online store on Shopify. And you want to embed your products on into your site to redirect people to buy on your Shopify store.

4. SamCart

You may feel that SamCart is just another website that makes it easy for you to sell online. Unlike Gumroad and Selz, SamCart has features that can help with boosting your sales. One of the features that I find interesting is their round up abandoned carts.

This feature gives you an idea on why people don't complete their sale. You can use the information to get them to complete their sale. Other e-commerce plugins like WooCommerce also has the same feature. But you can only get it as a premium extension. But this feature is already included in SamCart.

Another feature that caught my attention is their order bumps feature. It works the same like "You Might Also Like" section on Amazon. According to

SamCart, having this feature will help to increase your sales by 17%. WooCommerce also has the same feature like this. But it's only available as a premium extension.

With such cool features in SamCart, the pro plan costs $99 per month while the premium plan costs $199 per month.

Chapter Recap

You need to install an e-commerce plugin on your WordPress site if you want to create an online store. I recommend WooCommerce because of its many integration with other apps. You can also use a shopping cart plugin such as Gumroad to sell online. But a shopping cart is perfect for you if you only sell a handful of items. If you have a lot of items to sell, then it's better for you to install an e-commerce plugin.

CHAPTER 6

Getting a Premium WordPress Theme for Your Online Store

There are many free WordPress themes to choose from. And you can get it straight from the theme directory. In fact, they look as good as the premium themes. So, why I'm fussing you about getting the premium WordPress theme instead? Shouldn't the free one already do the job? Well, I wish that the free theme will do just fine. But that doesn't seem to be the case most of the time.

Maybe it has a lot to do with me being a picky online shopper. Even if you're not picky about how your website looks like, your customers do. In fact, they may decide whether to shop with you or elsewhere by judging on how your website looks like. If it looks ugly and unprofessional to their eyes, then they won't hesitate to shop elsewhere. I'm sure that you also did the same thing when you shop online.

Unprofessional-looking online store can make your business to resemble a scam. And that's the last thing you want your customers to portray you. The good news is premium WordPress theme can make your site looks professional. What's even better, the premium theme is already good enough on its own. So, you don't have to hire a web designer to get the professional look and feel for your online store.

What's even better, these themes can work well with an e-commerce plugin like WooCommerce. So, what about the other e-commerce plugins? Cart66 already stated clearly that the plugin is compatible with any WordPress themes. As for the other plugins, then you need to have a look at their website.

If you plan to use Jigoshop, then you can only find Jigoshop WordPress theme at their website.

Same goes with other e-commerce plugins like WP eCommerce and MarketPress. That's the reason why I highly recommend people to use WooCommerce for their online store. Apart from its stability, you have more choices for the premium theme for your online store.

But I don't have the budget to get the premium WordPress theme yet!
Well, I understand that you may not have the budget yet to get the premium WordPress theme. In fact, I was also thinking twice about getting a WordPress theme from Tokokoo which was on sale for $39 at that time! If you're in this kind of situation, it's alright to use the free WordPress theme for the time being.

But keep in mind that you don't have much flexibility when it comes to how you want your online store to look like. Unless you know HTML and CSS, then it's best for you to get a premium WordPress theme for your online store. Even if you know HTML and CSS, I still recommend you to get the premium theme. It takes less time for you to customize the look and feel of your website.

WordPress theme 101

Many WordPress themes consist of a framework and a child theme. The reason why WordPress theme has a separate framework and a child theme is simple. If you're planning to tweak your website's look, you only have to do the modification on your child theme. And the modification you do on your child theme will not affect the other functions of your website.

So, it's better for you to get a WordPress theme that has a separate framework and a child theme. Even if you don't plan to tweak your child theme, the framework can reduce the number of plugins you need to install. Too many plugins can slow down your website. And it doesn't help that the plugins may no longer work on your website after the plugin update.

Having a framework enables you to have the same features that you can get from the plugin. The only difference is the features are still working even after the theme update.

Where to get the premium WordPress theme, plus the free one

There are many places for you to buy the premium WordPress themes. But it's hard to get free themes that are compatible with the e-commerce plugins. So, you don't have much choice when it comes to the free

WordPress themes for the online store. The good news is the free one isn't that bad. And it also has a separate framework and a child theme too.

Let's have a look where you can get affordable premium WordPress themes. And if you're on a tight budget, I'll also show you where you can get nice-looking WordPress themes for free.

1. WooCommerce

What's the best place to get a free WordPress theme other than WooCommerce site, right? What I love about the themes on WooCommerce site is their framework is free. If you want to design the child theme on your own, then consider getting their Storefront framework.

They also have a wide variety of premium child themes to choose from. And each premium child theme will only cost you $39. Of course, they also have a few, decent-looking free child themes to choose from. WooCommerce site is the only place for you to get a free WordPress theme for your online store. I also used one of the free child themes from WooCommerce back then too when I got started.

2. Elegant Themes

Elegant Themes doesn't have a lot of premium WordPress themes for WooCommerce. But the one that you should be paying attention to is their Divi theme. You can design whatever looks you want with Divi without knowing any coding at all. If you're like me who gets bored easily with the current theme you have, then Divi theme is perfect for you.

I won't deny that Divi theme can be a bit difficult for you to grasp for the first time. If you can't decide on the look for your website, take a look at their pre-designed templates. And you can start working from there. That was what I did when I began to use Divi theme for the first time. It may take a while to get used to it. But Divi theme does give me the freedom that I need to create the desired look for my websites.

The only downside with Divi theme is you can't buy the Divi theme alone. You need to become Elegant Themes member if you want to get Divi theme. The personal plan will cost you $69 per year. It includes not only the Divi theme, but also other themes they create. You will also receive the theme updates and premium technical support as well.

Another option for you is to pay a one-time fee of $249. The one-time fee not only will give you the access to the whole theme archive. But you will also have complete access to all premium plugins and layered Photoshop files. I'm currently in the personal plan, but I'm planning to upgrade to the lifetime access since I love Divi theme so much.

In case you're wondering, Divi theme is the one I use in the sample store. Besides the sample store, I also use it on my website, The Efficient You and on my fiction author site, Sekina Mayu.

3. StudioPress

StudioPress doesn't have specific WordPress themes for the online store. But you can use Genesis Connect for WooCommerce if you want to use it for your online store. What makes their theme different is because of its framework, Genesis Framework.

With Genesis framework, your online store will be able to rank well in the search engines. It's all thanks to its clean, optimized code and its smart design architecture. The theme is also responsive, making it look good on any device. More importantly, it offers state-of-the-art, airtight security. With such security, it will make sure that no one will be able to exploit or take down your website.

You can buy Genesis framework alone for $59.95 or both Genesis framework and the child theme for only $129.95. If you get bored of your theme, you can only buy the child theme alone since you already have the Genesis framework. Depending on which theme you want to buy, you can customize the look and feel of your online store in any way you want. But it doesn't have the same kind of flexibility like Divi theme.

4. WPMU Dev

WPMU Dev only has one premium theme called Upfront. It has the same flexibility like Divi theme. But it's a lot easier to customize the theme compared to Divi theme. This theme is already included in your WPMU Dev membership. Upfront is also compatible with WooCommerce as well.

5. Obox Themes

Obox Themes is another place for you to buy premium WordPress themes. They also have many premium WordPress themes specifically for WooCommerce. Depending on what theme you choose, you have the option either to get a standard pack or premium pack. If you need prioritized support and advanced support help, then get the premium pack. The premium pack allows you to have technical support up to two years.

Besides premium WordPress themes, they also

develop WordPress plugins too. And these plugins are free and are accessible from the WordPress plugin directory.

6. Bluchic

If your target customers are mainly female, then Bluchic is a place that you should have a look. Unlike other premium WordPress themes I've seen, their themes do have this feminine look. So, it makes sense why their themes are perfect for the women-centric businesses. Their premium themes are also compatible with WooCommerce plugin too.

They also offer a service for setting up the theme like the one you see on the demo site. You can only qualify for this service if you purchase the premium theme from Bluchic. The service will cost you $79, but this price doesn't include revisions or customizations of the theme. The picture used in the demo site will be replaced by a gray placeholder instead.

They also offer free themes besides the premium theme. But I'm not sure if the free themes are compatible with WooCommerce or not. And you won't receive any support for the free theme other than the documentation provided.

7. ThemeForest

If you can't seem to find any themes that you like, maybe you can have a look at ThemeForest. It's a marketplace that sells premium themes and premium plugins. Most themes available are compatible with WooCommerce plugin. But there are a few premium themes that are compatible with WP eCommerce if you plan to use WP eCommerce.

Chapter Recap

There are many advantages of getting premium WordPress themes over the free one. For one, it can make your online store looks professional. And it can also minimize the WordPress plugins you need to install thanks to its framework. It's easy to customize too unlike the free one. With the free theme, you have to tinker the coding to get the desired look for your online store. If you'd like to save time, then it's best for you to get a premium WordPress theme.

CHAPTER 7

Accepting Payment at Your Online Store

In online shopping, your customers already expect that you accept payment online. So, it's obvious that you have to make it easier for your customers to pay you online. You can then proceed with processing their orders once you receive their payments. You can also use the payments to cover the shipping cost as well.

The easiest way to accept payment online

If you have been selling on eBay or Etsy, you already know that you need to have PayPal account. If you don't have PayPal yet, I highly recommend you to get one. Many customers love to shop in online stores that accept PayPal. If you don't offer PayPal as one of the payment methods, you're already missing out.

It's free to sign up for PayPal. Once you already sign up, you need to upgrade your account to business account. The business account allows you to receive the payments immediately. If you don't have a business account, you have to wait a few weeks for the payments to be available in your account.

Upgrading to the business account is free too. PayPal only charges you 2.9% + 30 cents for each transaction. So, it doesn't cost that much for using PayPal as one of the payment methods.

Accepting credit card payment

You need to have a payment gateway, SSL certificate, and a merchant account if you want to accept a credit card. Depending on the payment gateway you use, you have to pay fees for setting up the payment gateway. You also have to pay the charges for the credit card transaction as well.

Not all payment gateways are compatible with

your merchant account. So, your merchant account will depend on the location of your business operation. If you live in the United States, there are many payment gateways that you can use. But for the non-US businesses, you won't be able to use most of them. These payment gateways only cater for the US merchant accounts. In this situation, you can only use a payment gateway that caters to your country. It can be tough if your country doesn't have one.

The good news is there's another way for you to accept credit card payment. What's even better, you don't even need to have a merchant account, making it more appealing to small businesses. Some services are only available in certain countries. But there are also services that cater to pretty much every country you can think of.

1. PayPal Website Payment Standard

Upon payment, your customers will be redirected to PayPal website to pay you. They can choose to login and pay with PayPal or pay using a credit card. PayPal will be the one who will store your customers' credit card information for you. So, you don't have to worry about dealing with sensitive data like credit card information.

The credit card payment won't be available in an

instant. But it takes about 1-2 days for the payment to be available in your PayPal account. This is what I used for my online store back then since I don't have any other way to process credit card payment. And the payment gateway costs me a lot of money even for the setup alone.

The fee for processing credit card payment is the same as PayPal fees. But PayPal will charge you 3.9% + fixed fee per transaction for the international payments. The fixed fees will be charged in their local currencies.

2. Stripe

What I love about Stripe is not only it allows you to accept credit card payment. But they also allow you to accept other types of payment such as bitcoin, Alipay, and ACH Debits. Their processing fee is only 2.9% + 30 cents per transaction, which is perfect for those who are starting out. What's even better, you only need to link Stripe with your bank account. So, it's not necessary for you to have a business account if you want to use Stripe.

The only downside about Stripe is it's only available in certain countries. So, you need to check if your country is listed in Stripe before you can use it. You can also link Stripe with WooCommerce by using

Stripe extension for WooCommerce. The extension is available for free on WooCommerce site.

3. 2Checkout

2Checkout allows you to accept both credit card payment and PayPal. The payment processing pricing is depending on your business location. So, different countries will have a different payment processing pricing. You will also receive a volume discount if you process more than $50,000 a month.

You can only integrate 2Checkout with WooCommerce using the 2Checkout premium extension, though.

4. Paymentwall

Paymentwall works the same like 2Checkout. But unlike 2Checkout, you can only use Paymentwall with the shopping cart. And you can also accept other types of payment that are widely used in the customers' country. One of them is Alipay, which is China's third-party online payment app. Of course, Paymentwall also offers other types of payment besides Alipay. You can head over to their site to find out what other payment that you can accept with Paymentwall.

International businesses can receive the payouts

through bank, wire transfer and PayPal. You can also receive your payouts in check if you are based in the United States. But you can only receive the payout if you meet the $100 threshold. You will only receive your payouts once a month. But you can receive your payouts twice a month if your monthly revenues are more than $100,000 per month.

Their transaction fee is lower than PayPal. It only costs 2.7% + 30 cents for a transaction from the United States and 2.7% + 0.30 euro from the European countries. The transaction fees for other countries are 3.9% + 30 cents. They also don't have any hidden fees, setup fees and monthly payment for using their payment service.

You can integrate Paymentwall with WooCommerce. The Paymentwall extension is available for free at WooCommerce site.

Chapter Recap

PayPal and credit card are the preferred payment method when it comes to shopping online. So, you need to be sure that your online store accepts both types of payment. The simplest way to accept a credit card payment is to use PayPal Website Payment Standard. What's even better, you can use it regardless of where your business is based at.

Another way to accept credit card payment is to use 2Checkout or Paymentwall. That is if Stripe is not available in your country.

CHAPTER 8

Getting SSL Certificate for Your Online Store

You don't only need SSL certificate to process credit card payment. But you also need one if you're storing your customers' information on your website. It's understandable why they're worried about it. They don't want their personal data being compromised. They only want to be sure that their personal information is safe from the prying eyes. So, you need to ensure them that their sensitive data is encrypted and highly secured when they shop.

So, do you still need SSL certificate if you're using PayPal Website Payment Standard? Well, you don't need SSL certificate if you're using PayPal Website Payment Standard. But it's much better to have one. Having SSL certificate in place is proof that you're a legitimate business.

It doesn't matter what kind of service you use to process the credit card payment. You need to have SSL certificate in place.

The type of SSL certificate you should get
There are three different types of SSL certificates. And each of them has a different level of validation. The easiest SSL certificate to get is Domain Validation (DV) SSL certificate. This kind of SSL certificate only validates the domain ownership. It doesn't take that long for them to issue the SSL certificate to you. And you don't even need to submit any paperwork for the validation process. I had this kind of SSL certificate before when Fashion Paraizo was still with ProStores. Back then, they only offered one type of SSL certificate.

Another type of SSL certificate is Organization Validation (OV) SSL certificate. It's for websites that take customers' information such as login credentials. You should get this SSL certificate if you have a membership site. Unlike DV SSL certificate, paperwork is needed for the validation process.

Besides OV SSL certificate, there's also Extended Validation (EV) SSL certificate. This kind of SSL certificate has the highest level of validation. It also has the highest trustworthy feature, indicated by the green bar which you can see in the browser. With the green bar sign, it means that not only your website is secured. But it also proves that the company behind the site is a legitimate business. Like OV SSL certificate, you also need to submit paperwork for the validation process.

So, which SSL certificate you should get for your online store? Well, it's obvious that you should get EV SSL certificate. After all, you're going to process credit card information. And you will also store the personal information on your website. Doing so will ensure that scammers won't get a hold of your customers' sensitive data.

What you should do before getting SSL certificate

SSL certificate requires a different IP address if you want to host it on your server. So, you need to be sure that your hosting plan includes hosting SSL certificate.

If you're using Hostgator, you need to upgrade your hosting plan to Business Plan. It's the only hosting plan that offers a private SSL. You can then request the free private SSL by filling out the private SSL form request.

If you're using Bluehost for hosting your website, be sure that you have WooCommerce hosting plan. It's the only plan that already includes a dedicated IP for hosting an SSL certificate. Their shared hosting plan doesn't have a dedicated IP address. If you're in their shared plan, then you need to upgrade to their WooCommerce hosting plan.

It doesn't matter what hosting plan you use. You need to be sure that your hosting plan already includes a dedicated IP. You need it for hosting an SSL certificate.

Where to buy SSL certificate
There are many places to choose from when it comes to buying SSL certificates. Not to mention, there are many different brands to choose from as well. Does the brand matter in this case? Well, all I can say is different brands have different features for their SSL certificate. So, it all depends on what you want the SSL certificate to do for your online store.

One of the well-known SSL certificate providers

is Comodo. I never used Comodo before since I used GeoTrust SSL certificate back then. But one thing I love about Comodo is it's cheaper than GeoTrust. If you want an EV SSL certificate, Comodo is already perfect enough for your online store. But if you want more than the trustworthiness, you can get Symantec SSL certificate. But it will cost you $1,499 a year, though

If you're just starting out, Comodo EV SSL certificate is already good enough for your online store. Here are some of the places where you can get Comodo EV SSL certificate. But the price varies, depending on where you get it. So, expect that some of the places are cheaper from one another.

1. Hostgator

If you use Hostgator, you can buy it directly from your Hostgator customer portal. But the cost for their EV SSL certificate is $269.99 per year. But if you prefer to get the EV SSL certificate elsewhere, they can install it for you for only $10 per website.

2. Namecheap

Namecheap doesn't only sell domain names and WhoisGuard. But they also sell SSL certificates too. If you're looking for cheaper Comodo SSL certificate,

Namecheap is the best place for you. Like the domain names, they also have a special promotion for SSL certificates as well. But keep in mind that the renewal fee will follow the original price. Their Comodo EV SSL certificate costs $145 per year. You can get less than that during the promotion.

3. GoDaddy

Like Namecheap, you can also buy an SSL certificate at GoDaddy too. They also have special promotion from time-to-time. But the regular price for their SSL certificate is $199.99 per year.

Chapter Recap

You need SSL certificate not only for processing credit card payment. But you also need it to store customers' information on your site. There are many places where you can get SSL certificate. But be sure that your hosting plan has a dedicated IP address for hosting SSL certificate. You can then buy the SSL certificate and request your hosting company to install it for you.

CHAPTER 9

Creating Email Addresses Specifically for Your Online Store

You probably answer your customers' queries using your personal email address back then. It's okay to use your personal email address when you're selling on eBay or Etsy. But now, it's better for you to have a dedicated email address for dealing with your customers.

Not only will it make you look professional. But it

also gives reassurance to your customers that they're dealing with a legitimate person. It doesn't matter whether you're a well-known brand or not. It's not that hard to impersonate you online. And it's much easier to impersonate you if you're using free web-based email service like Gmail or Yahoo! Mail. Even if you're a solopreneur, it doesn't hurt to have a professional-looking email address.

The good news is it's not so hard to create an email address that has your domain name in it. In fact, you can create it as many as you want. That is as long as you check them all. What you need to do is to head over to your CPanel in your hosting account and starts creating one. The process for creating an email address is the same like how you create an email address in Gmail or Yahoo! Mail.

With how easy it is for you to create an email address that has your store name in it, you have no reason not to create one.

The email address you need to create
While there are no limits on how many email address you can create, it's still better for you not to go overboard. It can be a problem to manage them all, especially if you're operating the business on your

own. These are the email address that you need to create in your CPanel.

1. Support email

You may plan to use social media or live chat app such as Olark to answer your customers' queries. But it's still better for you to have a dedicated email for support. After all, only some people have social media accounts. And chat app like Olark still needs you to have a dedicated email address. They need to send you a notification should your customers contact you when you're offline. So, some of them prefer to send an email to get their queries answered.

Maybe it's only me, but I find it difficult to interact with the support on social media. I don't fancy sending many tweets only for sending my queries. Okay, maybe I should use Facebook or any other channels if I have a long, winded question. But then again, it can be too much if you're handling everything on your own. Using social media as a support can be daunting. It's especially true when you have so many people contacting you at the same time. Not only that, they expect a fast reply from you.

And that's the reason why it's recommended for you to create a support email address. You can manage the support email just fine on your own. That is as long as you notify your customers how long they expect you to get back to them. They don't expect to receive a reply from you the moment they send their queries to you.

Create this email address for handling your customers' support-related issues. You can also pass this support email to your virtual assistants or your employees. And let them manage the customers' queries on your behalf.

2. Personal email address with your store name on it

The purpose of this email is for contacting people who are related to your business. It can be your suppliers, anyone you meet in the networking party and influencers. Influencers tend to take you seriously if you're contacting them with this kind of email address. At least they know that they're dealing with a legitimate person from the company.

I always use this email address to contact potential people for collaborations. You don't need to have your email address known to your customers. You only let potential business partners and influencers know this email address. Emails still win when it comes to building a personal connection with someone.

3. Email used for sending on-going communications with your potential and existing customers

Some companies do mention that they don't track replies from that email address. That's usually the case for the email used for sending email newsletters. So, you should also do the same. You need to have an email dedicated for promotion only. You also need to make it clear that you don't track replies from that email address. Email marketing service like MailChimp allows you to set a reply email address. The replies then will go to a different email address instead of the one you use for sending promotions.

But that feature is only available for the paid account. The MailChimp's Forever Free plan doesn't have that feature. Otherwise, make it clear that you don't track replies from that email address.

How to access your emails

Accessing the emails is the same like how you would access your emails on Gmail or Yahoo! Mail. But then again, you need to go to your CPanel to access your email, though. It can be inconvenient, not only for you but also to your virtual assistant or your employees.

Besides, CPanel has everything related to your website, including your website files. So, it's not a good idea to let someone else accessing the emails through CPanel. After all, your CPanel contains confidential information about your site. And it's also hard to navigate the CPanel too. Even if you're the only one who is accessing the CPanel, you may prefer not to go there only for checking your emails.

Fortunately, there are many ways for you to access your emails without logging in to your CPanel. And what's the best part? You may already have it in your computer.

1. Microsoft Outlook

Some version of Microsoft Office also comes with Microsoft Outlook. If you have Microsoft Outlook installed, you can use it to check your email. Hostgator has a complete instruction on setting up your email account there. You can also use Microsoft Outlook to check more than one email account.

2. Mozilla Thunderbird

If you don't have Microsoft Outlook or you're using Mac, Mozilla Thunderbird is a good option for you. Not only it's free, but the email setup in Mozilla Thunderbird is a breeze too. It will begin to detect the configuration automatically after adding your email address. You don't even have to do the configuration manually. You can start receiving or sending emails as soon as the configuration is complete.

Mozilla Thunderbird is the email client I'm currently using to access my emails. I also send an email or reply back to the email from Mozilla Thunderbird as well.

3. G Suite

G Suite is formerly known as Google Apps for Work. With G Suite, you can create a custom email with your store name. Unlike the free Gmail, G Suite offers extra storage for your Gmail and Drive. They also guarantee 99.9% uptime. So, you don't have to worry about experiencing downtime whenever you want to send an urgent email to someone. On top of that, they also provide 24/7 phone and email support if you need help.

Hostgator has a complete instruction on how to setup Gmail account for your online store. The basic plan is $5 per user per month, and the business plan is $10 per user per month. You can try G Suite for 14 days for free if you're not sure if G Suite is perfect for your business or not.

Golden rules of email

For some of us, checking your inbox for the emails may not be a part of our lifestyle. And it's the last thing we want to do, especially when we're so occupied with the day-to-day operation. It's fine to let the emails piling up in your personal email inbox. But it's not okay when it comes to your business emails. After all, you may receive important emails through your business email address. If you don't reply the email on time, it will reflect your business in a bad way.

By all means, you have to set aside your time to check your inbox and also the time for replying the emails. You shouldn't be obsessed with your emails either. Striking a perfect balance can be hard. But with constant practice, you can handle it just fine.

Chapter Recap

You need to create a dedicated email account for your online store. You can do it by setting up the email account in your CPanel. You can then access the email accounts using Microsoft Outlook or Mozilla Thunderbird. You no longer have to access your CPanel only for checking your emails.

CHAPTER 10

Other WordPress Plugins You Should Install

You can still install other WordPress plugins in your online store. For the most part, it may not be enough with installing the e-commerce plugin by itself. The good news is you can still use these plugins alongside your e-commerce plugins. Some plugins are e-commerce-specific plugins. But you can use the rest of them regardless of what WordPress site you have.

Most WordPress plugins are free. But some

premium WordPress plugins also have a lite version too. The lite version of the premium plugins only has basic features, though. But then again, it's enough to give you a rough idea what these premium plugins can do for your website.

With so many plugins to choose from, it can be intimidating if you have no idea which one you should install. If you're using premium WordPress theme, then you don't have to install a lot of plugins. The framework itself already includes the features that you can get from the plugins.

Here are the plugins that I use on the sample store and also on my other WordPress sites. These plugins are free and available in WordPress plugin directory. It also works with any e-commerce plugin you use for your online store.

1. Akismet

Akismet is a plugin that can protect your blog from spam. This plugin is already installed during the WordPress installation if you use Hostgator. After activation, choose which plan that is best for your online store and retrieve the API key. Put the API key you get in the setting, and you're good to go.

The basic spam protection is free which is good enough for those who are just starting out. You can upgrade to the premium plan if you feel that your spam issue is getting out of control.

2. Google Analytics for WordPress by MonsterInsights
You may think that you don't need to install this plugin if you're using a premium WordPress theme. Most premium WordPress themes already include Google Analytics tracking in their framework. But if you want to track other metrics such as e-book download, then you need to install this plugin.

The premium version can track your ad campaigns and the e-commerce conversions. But you can use WooCommerce Google Analytics extension to track conversion instead.

3. iThemes Security
It's a plugin that can help with securing your WordPress site. With this plugin, you don't have to guess what you need to do when it comes to securing your website. It gives you a checklist of the things you need to do. The task is categorized by the most important things to the less crucial things.

This plugin also sends you a backup file of your website. You can then use it whenever your site crashes as a result of being hacked. The plugin doesn't guarantee that it will give 100% protection for your site. But at least it can help with reducing the possibility of your website from being hacked.

4. Limit Login Attempts

Sometimes, the hackers will use a combination of passwords to break into your site. You don't have to worry if you change the password during WordPress installation. But it can be terrifying when you have someone who tries to break into your WordPress site using brute force. This plugin will block the hackers after trying to hack your site after a few attempts. This plugin will give you extra protection when you use it alongside with iThemes Security.

5. WP SuperCache

This plugin can help with improving the speed and the user experience of your WordPress site. It also comes pre-installed when you install WordPress on your server.

6. Yoast SEO

This plugin will help you with on-page SEO. Not only can it give you suggestion on your on-page SEO effort. But it can also give you suggestion on your contents' readability. It works not only on the blog posts and the static pages but also on the product pages as well.

WooCommerce-specific plugins you should install

It's recommended for you to install these plugins as well if you're using WooCommerce. You can get these plugins for free through WooCommerce extension page in your online store or WordPress plugin directory. Keep in mind that you need to register on the plugin's website first before you can use it.

1. Olark

Olark is a live chat app for your site. Having a live chat app on your site will make it feels like having someone who greets and caters to your customers. But the difference is you're doing it in the virtual environment. On top of that, you can also see who's coming to your online store and what pages they're browsing at the moment.

Another thing that I love about Olark is you don't have to be present all the time. If you or any of your supports are not around, the customers can leave a message about their queries. You can get back to them whenever you're online. You can setup Olark on your phone or your computer through chat software such as Adium or Messages for Mac OS. You can also use Pidgin or Trillian if you're using Windows.

If you'd like to add the live chat feature on your website, place the code on the body of your site and you're good to go. But with Olark for WooCommerce extension, you don't have to put the code manually on your online store. You need to provide the extension with the Site ID, and you're good to go.

The pricing for Olark starts at $17 per operator per month. But they also have Free Forever plan. The Free Forever plan allows you to have one operator, 20 chats per month and the standard feature in Olark. Olark is the chat app I used when Fashion Paraizo was still online.

2. Paymentwall

Install this plugin if you're using Paymentwall to accept a credit card payment. They also provide a complete instruction on how to setup Paymentwall for WooCommerce.

3. PayPal Express Checkout

If you accept PayPal, then this WooCommerce extension is a must-have. By using this extension, the customers can skip the WooCommerce checkout process. And it will bring them straight to PayPal instead. This feature can improve the conversion up to 44%. What's even better, this feature is available in all countries. But you need to have PayPal Business account if you want to use this feature on your online store.

4. Stripe
Install this extension if you're using Stripe to process a credit card payment. Keep in mind that you need to have Stripe account before you can use it. And you also need to check with Stripe website if Stripe is available in your country or not.

5. WooCommerce Google Analytics
Do you still need it if your premium WordPress theme already has a tracking field for Google Analytics? Well, the answer is yes. Unlike the usual Google Analytics plugin, this extension enables e-commerce tracking. This extension allows you to see the conversion rate for your online store. And what products received the most traction in your online store.

Setting the e-commerce tracking in Google Analytics is already confusing enough. So, this extension makes it easier for you to do the e-commerce tracking. Otherwise, you have to configure the e-commerce tracking manually in Google Analytics. There's also a pro version for this plugin too if you need more insights for your online store.

6. WooCommerce PDF Invoices & Packing Slips

This plugin allows you to generate print invoice for your order. You can also customize your invoice too to enhance your store brand.

What about premium plugins? Do you need to have one?

It's hard to find out whether you ever need premium WordPress plugins or not. After all, it depends on what kind of business you have. Except for MarketPress and Cart66, it's not necessary for you to get them. After all, these premium plugins will only make your online store looks sophisticated. Other than that, it's not so much.

Some premium WordPress plugins do make things easier for you. For one, the 2Checkout WooCommerce extension will make it easy for you to use 2Checkout on your site. You can choose to integrate it without purchasing its WooCommerce extension. But it can be complicated if you try to do it yourself.

Keep in mind that you have to renew your plugin's license for the continuous support and update. You may think that you don't need the support. But you need the plugin update, so then it will stay compatible with the latest version of your

WordPress. Not only that, outdated plugins will make your online store prone to hackers too.

So, I won't brush off the importance of having premium plugins for your online store. If you'd like to buy premium WordPress plugins, these are the only plugins that I recommend you to have. They can save you tons of money and headache should something happened to your online store.

1. BackupBuddy

BackupBuddy allows you to back up your website content. Unlike the backup provided by iThemes Security, BackupBuddy backs up the whole site. You can set up the schedules whenever you want it to do backup for your site. Once it already backs everything up, you can set it where it should send the backup files to you.

Having a backup for your online store is critical since anything can happen to your online store. You'll never know that you can lose everything when someone hacks into your site. Not only that, you won't know that your site is being infected by malware. As a result, your customers can't visit your online store because of the malware warning.

The basic plan starts from $80 per year where it will back up one site. If you prefer one-time payment, you only have to pay $297. With a one-time fee, you can back up as many sites as you want. You'll also get lifetime plugin updates too.

2. iThemes Security Pro

Okay, you already get the free version of iThemes Security plugin. And the free version seems to be good enough for your online store. So, why you should get the pro version? Shouldn't the free version is good enough? Well, yes and no. It's true that the free version is already good enough. But if you want more protection, consider getting the pro version for your site.

The pro version has more features than the free version. But there are a few features that caught my attention the most. And they're two-factor authentication and scheduled malware scanning. The two-factor authentication requires you to enter the authentication code for your site. It works the same as Google's Two-Step Authentication. The two-factor authentication will prevent an unauthorized person from gaining access to your site.

As for the scheduled malware scanning, think of it like the antivirus program. It can help with detecting the malware at the early stage before it starts to infect the rest of your website. Malware can be malicious to your online store. So, you'd better prevent it before it spreads and Google begins to warn your visitors how dangerous your site is.

Buy what you need

For me, I think that the basic features of WooCommerce plugin are good enough for your online store. But you can always get other free and premium extensions that will benefit your business. Every online store has a different need. So, get the premium extensions if you think that it can boost your sales. You shouldn't get them for the sake of making your online store to look sophisticated.

After all, the premium extensions will increase your annual expenses. It's a different story if your online store generates a lot of sales on a monthly basis. But still, you shouldn't go overboard. These expenses will hurt your business if your sales are taking a dip out of sudden.

Chapter Recap

You can install other WordPress plugins to customize your online store. Some WordPress plugins also have premium plugins if you need more features. Keep in mind that different online store will have a different need. So, you should get the WordPress plugins that you think will help your business.

CHAPTER 11

Important Pages to Have On Your Online Store

Unlike selling on eBay, your customers have more opportunities to get to know more about you. With an online store, you can create a specific page for introducing your business. You can also create a page that jots down your business policies as well. And you can do that in greater details.

You can do this by creating a static page on your website. The good news is, it's not that hard to create a static page for your online store. The process for creating a static page is the same as creating a blog post. Unlike blog posts, it doesn't have a date stated on the page. And there's no comment section too.

These pages may not impact your sales in a direct manner. But some customers do use these pages as a part of their decision-making process. Here are the pages that you need to have in your online store.

1. Privacy policy page

Your customers want to know how you use their personal information. The last thing they want you to do is to sell their personal information to the third party. Crafting a privacy policy can be a daunting task unless you're a lawyer. But the good news is, there are many privacy policy templates you can use.

Use this privacy policy template to create a privacy policy page on your site. And it's free to use too. The only thing left for you to do is to format the page to make it more readable. The format can be messy when you paste it directly into your WordPress page.

2. Terms and conditions page

Terms and conditions page contains everything legal about your business. And that includes your return policy and privacy policy as well. If you're using WooCommerce, you have the option to link your Terms and Conditions page. So, your customers will see the page and have to agree with your terms during the checkout process.

I used the same one I had when I was still with Volusion. But like privacy policy page, they also have a template for terms and conditions as well. Just fill in the details, and you're good to go.

3. Return policy

If you don't mention how you handle returns, then the customers are going to make one for you. And for the most part, it's never favorable on your side. You should have this page in place, so then the customers know how you handle returns and what to expect if they want to return the items.

The policy statements don't have to follow what seems to be the standard practice in your industry. If you have the capability to process the return, then make it clear about the return procedure. If you can't process returns or the type of item you sell are not liable for returns, then you can offer a refund instead.

In my case, I don't provide return since all items that I have in store are pre-order items. So, I can't process the return for them. Instead, I offer them a refund if they find out that one of the items is defective. So far, I only processed one refund. For the most part, my supplier will make sure that none of the items are defective before they ship them to me.

4. Refund policy

If you plan to offer a refund instead, then make it clear how you intend to issue the refund. It can be a full refund or a partial refund. You also need to mention how long it takes for you to process the refund. In my case, I will only offer a refund for the defective items only. I won't refund the delivery cost.

Other ways for you to issue a refund is to refund it as a store credit. Some people are okay with this idea. But some of them seem to object if you refund it as a store credit instead. It doesn't matter how you plan to process the refund. You need to be clear what they should expect when and how you're issuing a refund.

5. FAQ page

Customers love to use the FAQ page as a way for them to get their questions answered. Create this page and list down the possible questions that your customers may want to ask you. You can also link your return policy and your refund policy in the FAQ page too. Your customers don't have to search for these pages if they're in one place.

You can use a website like Hosted Support if you can't come up with possible questions for your FAQ page. What I love about Hosted Support is they provide the FAQ template. All you have to do is to answer the questions given and delete other questions that may not be relevant to you. They also have a systematic return procedure in their module too if you're processing the return.

I've been using Hosted Support since my stint with ProStores. But since I don't feel like rewriting the FAQ again, I only link it on my WordPress header. The link will be redirected to my FAQ created on Hosted Support whenever customers click on it. Besides the FAQ, they also have the chat feature if you don't feel like signing up for the chat service like Olark. I prefer to use Olark since I can link my Olark with the chat software I use frequently.

6. Contact page

You still need to create this page even though you already create the necessary pages on your site. Sometimes, customers may have other questions that you don't cover in FAQ. They may also send you a query because they need a clarification from you. So, they'll be using this page to keep in touch with you.

Premium WordPress themes like Divi theme will make it easy for you to create a contact page. So, you don't need to install a contact form plugin if you want to create a contact page for your site. Besides the email support, you can also mention other ways for your customers to communicate with you. Be clear on how long it will take for you to respond back to them. At least they can expect when they will receive a reply from you.

7. About page

People prefer to do business with people that they know, like and trust. And the best way to do it is through your about page. You don't have to make it dramatic why you start your business. A simple reason for feeling frustrated that it's difficult for you to buy the things that you love will do.

If your business is also about supporting the cause that you believe in, don't forget to mention it too. People love to associate with businesses that are making a difference in other people's life. They also want to be a part of your cause too.

8. Homepage

It seems like a no-brainer when I mention that you have to create a homepage for your online store. Most premium WordPress themes already have a pre-designed template for the homepage. And they also offer many different designs for you to choose from. The only thing you need to do is to set it as a homepage in your WordPress setting. But if you're using Divi theme like I do, then you can either create one from scratch or use the pre-designed layouts.

9. Landing page

Unlike your homepage, the landing page is only for collecting your customers' information. For the most part, you'll use a landing page to collect the customers' email address. But you can also collect other details such as their birthday and the state they live. The landing page is more for people who are not yet becoming your customers. Once you already have their details, you can use it to build interest in your products. If you do this consistently, they may be turning into your customers.

10. Maintenance page

You can enable this page whenever your website is under maintenance. You can also enable this page if you're planning to launch or relaunch your online store. A premium WordPress theme like Divi allows you to create this page without the help of a plugin. I enable this page whenever I'm in the middle of revamping my online store, or I'm launching a brand new website.

Optional pages you can create for your online store

It's not necessary for you to have these pages in place. But having these pages will help you to stand out more than your competitors. You may find that these pages seem trivial to you and won't do much to please your customers. But don't be surprised that many businesses don't even have these pages in place.

1. Coming Soon page

Just because your brand new online store is under construction, it doesn't mean that you can only begin to tell people about it once it's up and running. You can start creating awareness about your online store by having the coming soon page in place. Depending on the premium WordPress theme you use, you can put the countdown timer on the page to get the visitors riled up for the grand opening.

But that's not the only reason why I'm suggesting you to create the coming soon page. You can also use it to build your mailing list. You can entice them to join your mailing list by offering a discount that they can use during your website's grand opening. You can also list your social media profiles on the page if you want. But I prefer to have an email opt-in form only on the page. You want them to do one thing, which is to join your mailing list.

2. Signup Thank You page

Some email marketing software like MailChimp already has it in place for you. But it's better to have your own version of the signup thank you page. Unlike the generic one that you can get in MailChimp, you can personalize the page to warm up your prospects and build trust with them at the same time.

3. Confirmation Thank You page

Your prospects will be redirected to this page after they already confirmed their email address. Email marketing software like MailChimp also has this page in place as well. But having your own confirmation thank you page will make them feel assured that they're already on your list. You can also add the incentive on this page as well. If you're offering a discount coupon, you can add it here. Don't forget to add the link to this page in the welcome email as well so they can access the incentive later.

Chapter Recap

If you want to gain your customers' trust, be sure that you have these pages on your online store. You may not realize it. But your customers do make a decision whether to shop with you or not by looking through at these pages alone.

CHAPTER 12

Configuring Shipping Rate for Your Online Store

When you sell online, how much you charge for shipping will either make or break your sale. You may not believe it, but people will decide to buy from you based on your shipping cost alone. Charge too little it will jeopardize your profit margin. Charge too much your potential customers will turn away from your online store.

If you are using WordPress, there are many

courier service plugins that will give you a live rate. So, you don't need to enter the shipping rate manually. But these plugins can only work if you are based in the United States. What about for those who live outside of the United States? Well, that's unfortunate. These plugins won't do much for you if you reside outside of the United States. So, the only thing you can do is to set up the shipping rate manually.

Sure, configuring the shipping rate manually can be time-consuming. But it allows you to be flexible on how you can charge your customers. Here are some of the ways you can charge your customers for shipping. And this method applicable regardless of what e-commerce plugin you use.

1. Price-based shipping

Many online stores charge their customers based on the amount they have in their cart. The higher the amount, the higher the shipping charge the customers have to pay. In most cases, the customers can qualify for free shipping if they spend more. For example, spend $100 and above to receive free shipping.

Price-based shipping is perfect for light items such as accessories and cosmetic. It's also ideal for those who are selling items that have low-profit margins. And can only make profits if the customers buy a lot. But this kind of shipping charge is not recommended if you're selling bulky items. It may put a dent in your profit margin if you attempt to use it for the bulky items unless it's for domestic shipping.

I used this type of shipping rate when Fashion Paraizo website was still live. In this case, the customers would get free shipping if their total order was $500 and above.

2. Weight-based shipping

Weight-based shipping is the most straightforward shipping rate to configure. All you need to do is to know the weight of the items and the shipping rate for each weight. All couriers will charge you based on the weight of the items. So, it doesn't need a lot of guesswork. You only need to estimate the weight of the items when you add the items in your online store.

If you are selling heavy and bulky items, then you should use this kind of shipping charge. Entering the shipping rate for this sort of shipping charge can be tedious. Depending on the items you sell, it takes a long time to setup compared to price-based shipping.

And if you're not careful, the shipping rate for the total order may not even show up. It happens when the customers' order exceed the weight in your shipping configuration.

I also used this shipping configuration when I was still on ProStores and Volusion. I was able to use this shipping configuration when I made a switch to WooCommerce. At that time, I used a free plugin called AWD Weight/Country Shipping. It's too bad that you can no longer use this plugin with WooCommerce latest updates.

3. Per-item based shipping

It works similarly like price-based shipping. But it charges the customers based on the number of items in the cart. So far, I've yet to come across any online store that offers this kind of shipping configuration.

4. Shipping based on shipping class

This sort of shipping charge requires a few settings to make it work. For one, you will create a few different classes, and each class has its own shipping rate. Amazon uses this kind of shipping charge where they charge you based on the type of items you purchased. So, you will know the actual shipping rate for your items after determining the weight for the item class.

This kind of shipping configuration is perfect if you are selling both light and heavy items.

The current version of WooCommerce allows you to set this sort of shipping rate. I won't deny that it can be confusing at first. But it's a lot easier and faster to setup than weight-based shipping configuration. What you need to do is to identify the shipping class from your items. And estimate the weight of one item in that shipping class. From there, you can use the weight of the item to determine the shipping rate for the shipping class. Repeat for other shipping class you set in your online store.

It's not hard to identify what shipping class you should create. In my case, I created the shipping class based on the product category. Fashion Paraizo is selling clothes. So my shipping classes are dresses, bottoms, shoes, handbags, accessories, tops, and outerwear. From there, it won't be so hard to identify the shipping rate. You only need to estimate the weight of one item from each shipping class. Use that shipping rate when you configure this type of shipping configuration.

Even if you don't use WooCommerce, I still think that you should pick this shipping configuration. It's because it's easy to set up, especially when you ship internationally.

Shipping internationally

Processing international orders are different than processing domestic orders. And it can be tricky too. It's especially true if you have never shipped anything commercial internationally before. Unlike domestic shipment, you need to prepare more documents for the international shipment. If you don't have these documents ready, you may not be able to ship the items to your customers in that country.

The good news is you don't need to worry so much about what documents you need to prepare. All couriers will provide the guidelines for preparing documents for the international shipments. Each country has its own legal document preparation for the item clearance. But that shouldn't be your concern as long as you follow what the courier told you to do. It shouldn't be a problem as long as you have everything the courier requested.

You should also inform them that they need to pay for duty import and tax should their parcels are on hold by the custom. You also won't attempt second delivery if they don't claim the parcels or the courier returns them back to you. In this situation, their orders will not be refunded.

Clear shipping terms will make things easier for

the international customers. You can also use the same conditions to the domestic orders too if you find it applicable.

Getting lower shipping rates for your online store

It's possible to get a lower shipping rate for your online store. You can do so by opening up a corporate account with the courier. With a corporate account, not only you will get a shipping discount. But you can also pay the shipping charge later. You only need to pay them once they confirmed that they already delivered the shipments. They will also provide shipping supplies and allows you to schedule your shipment pickup too.

But then again, your shipping discount will depend on the volume of your shipment. So, it can be hard to get a deep discount shipping rate if you don't have a lot of shipping volume. If the discount isn't that different from the counter rate, then you don't need to get a corporate account. Another way for you to get a deep discount rate for shipping is to use order fulfillment service. I will cover about it in the later chapter.

Offering free shipping

Free shipping seems like a norm these days. In fact, some stores get more sales when they offer free shipping. They think that it's a better investment than generating sales through advertising. So, it's understandable that you're also tempting to offer free shipping too. And it seems like a perfect strategy even if you're a brand new online store.

But then again, offering free shipping isn't a unique strategy. Some online stores can do it because they have a deep discount shipping rate. It may seem like offering free shipping will cut their profit margins. But since they have a large shipping volume, it won't become a problem for them.

I know it can be too much for you to offer free shipping when you're not making a lot of sales yet. So, should you abandon the idea of offering free shipping? If you still want to offer free shipping in your online store, then my suggestion for you is to do it in stages. Once you already have a large shipping volume, you can then do the same for other places or country zone.

Don't feel intimidated either if your competitors are offering the free worldwide shipping. Instead, offer free nationwide shipping with conditions like with orders $100 and above. This approach will give you a glimpse on offering free shipping. You can start offering free worldwide shipping after that. You can offer the free shipping based on which country you receive the most orders.

To be honest, it's not a compulsory to have free shipping. It only puts you on the advantage. If free shipping seems farfetched to you, then you should be offering something else that won't cost so much. Offering a free gift is one of the strategies you can use. But then again, it may not be convincing enough for your customers to shop at your online store. What drives them to shop with your competitors in the first place is still the free shipping option.

Offering free shipping can be costly. But from the customers' perspective, it's the most alluring things. They can spend extra on anything. But somehow, they refuse to spend their money on shipping, if they can help.

Chapter Recap
Your shipping rate configuration is depending on what you sell. But if you can't seem to decide which one you should use, then opt for the shipping based on the shipping class. It's easier and faster to setup. You can use this sort of shipping configuration regardless of what you sell. You can even use this

kind of shipping to set free shipping for your online store. Free shipping is a perfect way to get people to shop with you. But you need to do it in stages so then this offer doesn't rub off your profit margin.

CHAPTER 13

Writing a Product Description That Sells

You already know that many people are visiting your online store through Olark. Just to recap, it's the live chat that you installed on your online store. You can see what they're browsing with Olark. You notice that they come across this product. They stay there for a while. You thought that they might click the add-to-cart button. But it seems like they don't. What's going on here?

Well, it's nothing to freak out when they don't buy anything when they come to your online store. That's always the case if it's their first visit. It's hard to pinpoint the exact reason why they don't want to buy from you. But we can assume that the reason has something to do with your product description.

In the online world, customers can only rely on the product description to find out more about the products. If you write a thorough product description, chances are they may likely to buy the products from you. And it's still applicable even if the things that you sell are also available offline. Customers love to conduct their research online and complete their purchases offline. So, it makes sense why your product description plays a significant role in the sales conversion.

How to write a product description that sells

The good news is writing a product description that sells isn't as hard as you thought. And it's not a rocket science either. But keep in mind that it takes a lot of time when it comes to writing a good product description. With practice, your product description writing will improve with time. From there, you can start to create a template to make the writing much faster.

Before you do anything, it's better for you to learn as much as you can about the products you're selling. It's hard to write about the product if you don't know what the product is all about. Imagine yourself selling the same product door-to-door. You can't expect people to buy from you if they don't know anything about the product. You can't expect them to read the description at the back of the item either. Well, that is if the product has one. If you're selling clothes like I did, there's nothing to describe the clothes other than the tag attached to it.

So, do what you can to know more about your products. You can do so by visiting the manufacturer's website. You can also use their brochure and their catalog, if any, to learn more about the products. These resources can help with deepening your understanding about the products you sell.

Writing a product description will vary by business. So, here's the general guideline for writing a product description.

1. Identify what the product is all about
The first thing that the customers want to know is what the product is all about. Once they already know about it, they may choose to read the product

description or hit the back button. Don't worry if the customers are hitting the back button. It's better that way. At least they already know that the product is not for them before they add it to their shopping cart. The last thing you want is they return the item only because they purchased the item that doesn't suit them at all.

2. Explain how the features of the product will benefit them

What gets people to buy the products have a lot to do with how the products will help them. People won't be so motivated to buy by features alone. And they don't care even if they're better than the competitors' products. If you want to persuade people to buy, then you have to explain to them how the product will benefit them. They're more likely to buy if they know in what way the product will help them.

Let's say you're selling cosmetics online, and one of the new items is mascara from a well-known brand. And it has a one-of-a-kind, zig-zag, mascara brush. In this case, you shouldn't describe what's so fascinating about the brush. You should say that the unique brush makes mascara application easy. And it helps to lengthen the eyelashes, giving a falsie effect. Explain the benefit to them, and they're more likely to buy from you.

Customers can't be bothered with the cool features if they can't see how the product will benefit them.

3. Emphasize who should be buying the product

Make it clear who should be buying the product. If you do that, they're less likely to make the wrong purchasing decision. And you can avoid getting returns for this product too. Going back with our mascara example, you can say that this mascara is perfect for the beginner. And it's also for those who like to have long lashes without having to wear a falsie.

4. Let your customers know what result they should expect

If you're selling products that will produce a specific result, tell them about the end result. Don't forget to add the disclaimer that the results aren't typical. If you don't, they may attempt to sue you because they didn't get the result that you described. In our mascara example, you can say that the end result is natural-looking long lashes. And it looks like they're wearing falsies.

5. Add other important details that will help with their purchasing decision

It can be things like extra photos and a full list of ingredients. It can be anything that can help customers to come up with their final decision. What seems unimportant to you may be important to your customers. Just put everything that you think that the customers may need. You can always add more information based on the queries that your customers sent to you.

Should the product description be short or long?

There are no general rules when it comes to writing a product description. Sure, a long product description will convert better. But a short product description can convert as good as the long one. So, the length of the product description won't matter. Just be sure that it covers everything your customers need to know about the product.

What you shouldn't do

You may not have the time to do your due diligence when it comes to writing a product description. So, you end up copying everything from the manufacturer's website. You don't have the time to write it from scratch. Sure, the manufacturer doesn't mind at all that you're copying the product description.

It's okay to copy the product description right away from the manufacturer's website. But your customers may already see the same product description everywhere they go. And they may expect that you will give the same product description like everyone else.

If you're the customer, does the same product description will help you with the buying decision? Of course, it won't. It's a different story if your product description is different and a lot better than everyone else. And the only way to do that is to write it from scratch. Sure, it's time-consuming. But if it can help with your sales, then it's worth doing it after all.

Chapter Recap

If you want to write a product description that converts, you need to put yourself in the customers' shoes. By doing that, you'll get a brief idea on customers' purchasing behavior which leads them to buy more from you. The product description doesn't have to be long. It should provide enough information that prompts them to buy from you.

CHAPTER 14

Managing Your Orders

Regardless of which e-commerce plugin you use, it's not that hard to view and manage the orders you receive. For the most part, you can see the orders you received directly from the dashboard. It should look familiar to you if you're selling in a marketplace like eBay, Amazon, and Etsy.

Managing your orders from the dashboard will be okay if you only receive a few orders a day. Even if you have a lot of order volume in a month, it's still bearable to manage these orders from the dashboard alone. But what if you receive hundreds of orders a day? With such a high sales volume, you need to keep an eye on your inventory too. What items are moving fast and need a back order? What to do with slow-moving items?

The good news is your online store dashboard won't crash if you receive a huge amount of orders in a day. But it can be difficult for you to process the orders in a speedy manner by relying on the dashboard alone. As a retail business, you want to make sure that you process the orders on time and without any errors at all. At the same time, you want to be sure that the customers get what they order. You don't want to delay with processing their orders because of the back order.

I admit that the situation itself can be far-fetched if you're just starting out. But it doesn't hurt for you to prepare ahead of time with this amazing tool. Sure, it does have an upfront cost. If you want to increase the efficiency of your order process, it's better to do so while you have a small volume of orders. You may not have the time to learn on how to use it properly once your online business starts to kick in.

So, what software I'm talking about here? The tool that I'm referring to is order management software. This software goes beyond what your online store dashboard is capable of.

What order management software does?

One of the things that you need to do as soon as you receive the orders is to print the required documents for shipping. For domestic shipments, a shipping label will be enough. But for the international shipments, you need to add a commercial invoice. With order management software, you can process the orders in bulk.

All order management software has a direct link to the courier's live rate. So, you can submit the shipping information and schedule the pickup at the same time. You can do these processes straight from the order management software itself. What's even better, these order management software offer discounted shipping rate. So, you don't have to charge your customers a lot for shipping. It can also make offering free shipping to your customers possible too.

Order management software is also handy if you're selling in other sales channels. Maybe you're also selling on eBay, Amazon, and Etsy. You know how painful it is to manage the orders on a separate dashboard. With order management software, you can manage all orders in a single place.

You can also use the order management software for processing offline orders too. So, it makes things easier and speedier for you to manage your orders. If you're accepting returns for your online store, this tool will make managing returns a lot easier as well.

What these order management software don't do
Keep in mind that you still need to pay the shipping couriers you use to ship your items. Your subscription doesn't include the shipping rate for each item you ship. The best part is you can pay them directly from the order management software.

The right time to start using order management software
There's no right time when it comes to using the order management software for processing orders. So, I can only suggest you to start using it when your order volume starts to pick up. Perhaps you can start using it when you receive a few orders a week on a consistent basis.

All order management software has a free trial. So, you can take this opportunity to test drive the tool before you become fully committed to it. Some order management software charges you based on your order volume. So, you need to choose which order volume that is close to your business. If you feel that the tool may not help you much, then you can stop using it after your trial period is over.

Recommended order management software you should be using

There are many order management software for you to choose from. And this software has its own pros and cons. Another problem is you may not be able to use it if your business is outside of the United States. If this is you, then you're out of luck. Luckily, you can use order management software even if you live outside of the United States. Here are some of them, which they're web-based order management software.

1. Order Cup

Order Cup has everything you need to manage your orders. What's even better, Order Cup allows you to process your orders even if you don't live in the United States. It's all thanks to its international origins feature. This feature lets you get a live shipping rate from couriers like FedEx or UPS in your country.

You can integrate your online store with Order Cup if you're using WooCommerce. Of course, you can only do the integration if you already have a registered account with Order Cup. The Order Cup WooCommerce extension is free. And you can get it from WooCommerce extension page.

Order Cup's pricing starts from $20 per month for businesses who process 500 shipments per month. All plans allow you to gain access to all carriers' live rate. But if you want custom templates for invoices and packing slip, the price starts from $40 per month.

So, should you be using Order Cup even if you live in the United States? Well, absolutely, especially if you want everything automated for you.

2. ShipStation

ShipStation works the same like Order Cup. But their lowest tier is only $9 per month. And it allows you to manage 50 shipments per month for all selling channels. ShipStation is perfect if you'd like to give order management software a try because of its low cost. But you can only use ShipStation if your shipments are originating in the United States.

You can integrate ShipStation to your WooCommerce store with WooCommerce extension. The ShipStation WooCommerce extension is free. You can get the extension from WooCommerce website.

3. ShippingEasy

What I love about ShippingEasy is that they have a free tier that allows you to ship up to 50 packages per month. The free tier also receives low shipping rates. But if you want even lower shipping rates, you need to sign up for the paid plan. The basic plan starts from $29 per months for businesses with shipments up to 500 packages per month. Like ShipStation, you can only use it if your shipments are originating in the US.

You can also integrate Shipping Easy to your WooCommerce store with WooCommerce Extension. It's available for free at WooCommerce website.

4. Stamps.com

Stamps.com allows unlimited shipments, unlimited sales channels, and unlimited live telephone support. What's even better, you only pay $15.99 per month. There are no hidden costs, and you can cancel anytime. If you've decided to give them a try, you'll receive free USB Shipping Scale which you only pay $5 for the postage.

The only downside to using Stamps.com is they only offer USPS as their main shipping courier. If you prefer to use other couriers, then your best bet will be to use Order Cup, ShipStation or Shipping Easy.

You can only use Stamps.com if your business is based in the United States.

You can also integrate Stamps.com with your WooCommerce store. But Stamps.com WooCommerce extension will cost you $79 per year, though.

5. ShipRobot

Just like ShippingEasy, ShipRobot also has a free tier. Their free tier allows you to process shipments up to 25 shipments per month. With ShipRobot, not only you can connect to more online marketplaces such as Storenvy. But they also offer other shipping couriers too such as Canada Post and Swiss Post.

If you need more features, then you can upgrade to their paid tier. Their paid tier starts from $20 per month and allows you to manage 300 shipments per month. What I love about ShipRobot is their highest tier (Gobot plan) only cost $60 per month. And it allows you to manage unlimited shipments. If you already have a high sales volume, their Gobot plan is worth getting for your business.

You can connect ShipRobot to your WooCommerce through API. ShipRobot also allows shipments originating from outside of the United States. But it's only limited to Canada and Europe.

6. Ordoro

Ordoro's order management system will make it easy for you to manage items that you sell in a bundle. It doesn't matter how complex is your bundling scenarios, Ordoro can manage the inventory for you. You can also use Ordoro for managing drop shipping orders too.

Their basic tier is only $25 per month, which allows you to manage 500 orders per month. But they also have a starter plan where you can use it to manage up to 50 orders per month, one sales channel, and one user. Like ShippingEasy, you can only access much cheaper rate if you sign up for the paid plan.

Just like ShipRobot, you can also connect your WooCommerce store to Ordoro by using API.

7. Shippo

The way Shippo works is different than any other order management software I've come across so far. In Shippo's case, it only helps you with finding the best shipping rates. And you can only print the shipping labels after you pay the shipping courier of your choice. So, you can ship as many as you want. It doesn't even have monthly fees, setup fees, and cancellation fees. The only thing you have to pay is the shipping cost and an extra 5 cents.

Shippo is perfect for you if you don't like the idea of paying monthly fees. And you don't need anything fancy for your order management software. It's a simple solution for managing your orders. What's even better, you can also use Shippo even if your business is based outside of the United States.

You can connect Shippo to your WooCommerce store by using API. If you sign up for Shippo through WooCommerce link, you don't have to pay label fees for 90 days.

Chapter Recap

Order management software will make your order processing becomes faster and more efficient. You can start using it even when you don't have a lot of orders coming in. So, you can use the time to get yourself familiarized with it. Keep in mind that only a few of them can handle orders from the international origins. So, you need to check with them first before you sign up with any of them.

CHAPTER 15

Shipment Packaging for Your Online Store

If you're selling on eBay and Etsy, you may not pay much attention to the packaging you use for sending the items. For all you know, you can use a tissue box since it's sturdy enough for your shipment. But if you don't, you're maybe using the shipping mailers or boxes provided by the courier.

Unlike eBay or Etsy, your customers expect you to send their items in a nice-looking shipping box.

And they may not mind much if it's the shipping box you use is the one provided by the courier. Other than that, it looks unacceptable to them. Using a tissue box or any recycled box for that matter will only make you look unprofessional.

Customers in places like eBay and Etsy don't mind about the packaging you use. They know that people who are selling on these marketplaces are mostly individuals. Sure, there are big businesses who are selling on eBay. But the customers who are shopping on eBay don't have a huge expectation on you. They only care about processing their orders right on time.

So, it's important to have a proper packaging for your online store. Whether you like it or not, customers tend to judge you not only on your web design but also on your packaging too. So, using a recycled box or a tissue box as a packaging for your shipment won't cut it. You can say that you're doing it out of the environment concern. But it looks more like you're cutting corner.

What you should do instead
You may not face this kind of problem if you have a corporate account with the courier company. After all, they will provide you with the shipping supplies

needed for your business for free. But if you don't have any account with them, you won't get any shipping supplies. It's also the same if you're using order management software like Order Cup. You still need to use your own packaging to send the items.

The good news is you can buy shipping boxes from a website or a store which sells shipping supplies. They have a lot of shipping boxes in different sizes to choose from. So, you can buy whichever size that suits your business. They also sell bubble wrapping and document holders too. You need a document holder for placing your packing list and the commercial invoice. Depending on the quantity, you tend to get a better price if you buy in bulk.

But what if you want to have a customized packaging for your online store? Is it only applicable to a giant company like Amazon? Well, you can have that too. The best part is, it won't cost arm and leg. It costs a bit more than the shipping box you get in the shipping supplies store or website. So, expect to pay premium price if you want to get customized packaging for your online store.

Getting a customized packaging not only will make you look professional. But it can also enhance your store branding even further. So, get them if you feel that the normal shipping box is a bit blah to you and won't do any justice to your brand.

The best place to get customized packaging for your online store

Getting a customized packaging for your online store isn't as hard you think. Here are some of the places for you to get a customized shipping box for your online store.

1. Packlane

Packlane offers a customized shipping box for your online store. All you need to do is to choose which type of box you want and start designing the box in any way you want. You can also get a quote right away if you want to know how much you expect to pay for your customized shipping box.

What I love about Packlane is they have a high-quality printing for the box. And they also allow a small minimum printing too. With Packlane, you can order as little as ten boxes. What's even better, the cost per box is low too, even for ten boxes. The cost per box will become lower the more boxes you order.

Another thing that I love about Packlane is they also ship internationally. But they admit that it may cost a lot to get the boxes shipped to you. They suggest that you should check the shipping rate before you submit your order.

2. Lumi

Like Packlane, Lumi also allows you to design your own shipping boxes. What's amazing about Lumi is they don't only offer customized shipping boxes. But they also offer other types of packaging such as mailers and bags. You can choose to buy them either blank or with the custom design. They also sell shipping supplies such as tapes, thermal shipping labels, crinkle paper, tissue paper, hang tags and butcher paper. What's even more amazing, you can also customize your supplies with your brand if you like.

The only downside about Lumi is you can only buy the packaging in case. And you can't mix the designs and sizes to meet the minimum quantity. Depending on the quantity, the price per case will become lower the more cases you buy. You can always contact them to let them if you need lower quantity for your order. Keep in mind that they have a different pricing for the blank packaging and the custom packaging.

They also ship internationally too. But the freight cost will be expensive since you have to buy these packaging and supplies in bulk.

The steps you need to do to get a customized packaging for your online store

Here are the things that you need to do before submitting your order to Packlane or Lumi. Keep in mind that you can always redesign your shipping boxes at any time. You don't have to live with the current design for the rest of your life.

1. Identify the type of packaging you need

The type of packaging you need will depend on what items you're selling. If you're selling lighter items, then you need to get a mailer box. It's a small box which resembles the pizza box. You can adjust the dimension you need during the design process to suit your need. Another option is to use mailers. It can be either the poly mailers or the Kraft mailers.

Another packaging you can get is the classic carton which is a paperboard box. You can get this box if you're selling a large but light item. If you're selling clothes like me, then your best option is to use mailers. You can use this box if your customers buy a lot from you. But if you're selling bulky and heavy items, get a shipping box that is thicker than the paperboard box.

If you already have a decent amount of sales volume, then it won't be hard for you to decide on what type of packaging you need. If it's your first time selling online, then it's better for you to get all kinds of packaging in a small quantity. From there, you can see which packaging you need the most.

2. Determine the type of cardboard you want for your shipping box

Keep in mind that different type of cardboard will give you a different finishing result. If you love dark and bold color on your shipping box, then the Kraft corrugated board is perfect for you. But the Kraft corrugated board won't have the same color intensity like the one you see in the online proof.

But if you want the colors to pop, then pick white corrugated board instead. This type of board works great for all color, especially the lighter ones. It will also give you the same color intensity as the one in the online proof.

3. Get your store logo in order

If you already have a professionally-designed store logo, use it on your packaging. If you don't, then you need to get it done. Not only you need the store logo for your packaging. But you also need it for your website and printed materials. It can be things like your receipt, commercial invoice, and packing list.

You don't have to be a graphic designer to design your own logo. The best way for you to design a store logo is to use a text-based logo. It's easy for you to do even with a minimal design skill. You can start design your store logo using free graphic software such as Canva. It has many beautiful and professional-looking fonts for you to choose from. And it's also perfect for beginners too.

Canva is my go-to place whenever I need a quick graphic design for my blog post and social media graphics.

4. Decide on the pattern and the color palette you want on your packaging

If you prefer a single color on your packaging, then you may skip this part. But if you want to have pattern on your packaging, then you need to decide on what kind of pattern you want. The good news is you don't need to design your own pattern if you choose to have one on your packaging.

If you'd like to buy a customized pattern for your shipment packaging, I highly recommend Creative Market. They offer tons of patterns that are licensed for the commercial use.

5. Decide on how many packaging you plan to order

If you can't seem to decide on the amount, then settle for the minimum order. Packlane allows you to order ten boxes for each type, so that should be good enough. You can always place the order again if you're running out of the boxes.

Chapter Recap

You can't use any type of boxes for your shipment since customers have a high expectation for your online store. If you find using the plain box seems blah to you, then you can get a customized, branded packaging from Packlane or Lumi. You can buy as little as ten boxes from Packlane. The price per box will become lower if you buy more. Same goes with the packaging you can get from Lumi.

CHAPTER 16

Order Fulfillment Service for Your Online Store

Your online store is live, and you're ready to take orders. You even already ordered a few shipping boxes with your store name on it. Once the orders come in, you need to ship them out. Initially, you don't mind to do the order fulfillment yourself. As your business starts to grow, you begin to hire a few people to do the fulfillment for your online store.

But after a few months, your business starts to

grow even larger. And you end up having these workers to do overtime only to get the shipments out of your house. You also need to rent a warehouse since you already outgrow the space in your garage. You also want to stock more items since the demand for that product in your online store is growing larger. And your employees will have a better working environment if they work in a warehouse.

Congratulations if your business is growing at such pace. Having your own warehouse to do the fulfillment can be good for your business. But there's also another option for you. And it's far simpler than renting a warehouse. Enter the order fulfillment service.

What order fulfillment services can do for your online store

It depends on which order fulfillment service you're working with. But all order fulfillment service will fulfill your customers' orders on your behalf. They can also be the one who will receive your items from the suppliers. In other words, they handle the backend side of your business on your behalf.

They also help with processing returned items if your store accepts returns. Some order fulfillment services also offer gift wrapping for your business too. Order fulfillment service isn't that different from warehousing. The only difference is you don't have to rent a warehouse, hire and train staffs for doing order fulfillment.

Benefits of using order fulfillment service
Order fulfillment services receive a large shipping volume on a daily basis. So, they get a deep discount, allowing them to offer affordable shipping rate to you. If your sales volume isn't big enough to qualify for a deep discount, then consider using this service.

Since they have tools like a weighing scale, you can rest assure that you'll get an accurate weight for your items. That saves you from making a wrong estimate about the item weight. And you don't have to worry so much about how to pack the items because they can handle those things for you. For the most part, they already have the packaging for shipment covered for you. But if you insist on using the customized shipping boxes, then you can inform them about it.

You can also make full use of their storing facilities if you already outgrow the space in your house. You can choose to rent their storage as many as you want. With such flexibility, you don't have to limit how many items you can stock for your online store. Now you can think about scaling your business since you don't have to worry about the item storage.

Some order fulfillment services also let you hire their staffs to cater for your business. It's the same like hiring your own staffs for the order fulfillment. But this time, the staffs are from the order fulfillment service itself. So, you don't have to worry about training them. They already know what to do. It can also make the communication a lot easier since they're managing your orders only.

Large order fulfillment services usually have a few warehouses across the globe. So, you can store your items in any warehouse location you prefer to reduce the shipping cost. You can do that if you have a high sales volume coming from that country or nearby countries.

What you need to consider before hiring order fulfillment service

Each order fulfillment services have different ways of doing things. So, it's best for you to find an order fulfillment service that suits your business. Here are some considerations before hiring order fulfillment service for your business.

1. How much they will charge you for their service

Most order fulfillment service will charge you a certain amount per item. But there are also a few of them that charge you on a monthly basis regardless of your order volume. This kind of order fulfillment service usually has an online calculator. You can use it to estimate how much you will be paying per month based on your order volume.

As for the per item charge, they usually don't publish their rate on their website. But they will provide you with the rate when they're sending a proposal to you.

2. Do they handle pre-order shipments

You need to be upfront with them if your business is based on the pre-order model. Some order fulfillment services, usually the large one don't cater to this kind of business model. So, you need to find one that can cater to your business.

3. How they handle returned items

Some order fulfillment services would issue RMA on the packing list. And if the customers decided to return the items, they will use the RMA as a reference for you and them. But some order fulfillment services would want you to issue the RMA yourself. If you have to issue RMA, you need to find a way to integrate this with your order fulfillment service.

If you're using the return ticket system from Hosted Support, it will generate the RMA for you. Use this RMA to notify the order fulfillment service about the returned items.

4. What other services they offer

Some order fulfillment services may not list down what else they do on their website. They will only list down their other services in their proposal. So, it's up to you to decide whether you want that extra services or not. If you need other services such as gift wrapping, you need to ask them if they provide such services.

Some order fulfillment services do have services like gift wrapping. But they may want you to provide the gift wrapping materials yourself.

5. How long it takes for them to process the order

I believe it's the most important question you need to ask to your order fulfillment service. If they take a long time to process your customers' order, it will jeopardize your business. That's always the case when the customers expect to receive the items in a given period. They would say that they will process the orders within 24 hours. But you can only pray that they did process the orders within 24 hours.

A similar situation did happen to me before. Back then, I was dealing with the order fulfillment service based in the United States. The sales director told me that they would get the items shipped less than a week. Their process would involve 1 to 2 days to get the items barcoded if my items weren't barcoded. And it would take 1 to 2 days for the items to be available in their fulfillment system. They would ship them within 24 hours after that.

Instead, they shipped the items three weeks after it arrived at the facility! It seemed that it took almost one week to get my item barcoded. They also needed another week for the item to be available in their system for order fulfillment. As a result, the customers refused to buy from me anymore. They even unsubscribe from my newsletter when I sent an email newsletter to them.

It seems that my business wasn't the only one who was experiencing such terror. Even a large business like Zappos had a similar experience too. It happened before they have their own facility in Las Vegas to fulfill the orders. Like me, they were also sold with a similar idea and faced more or less the same situation as me.

What was even worst, they lost more than half of their stocks at the same time. It happened when the truck which carried their stocks got involved in an accident. As a result, their shoes were scattered, and they could never recover the lost inventory. It must be hard for them when they had to delay the fulfillment because they lost some of their inventories.

Okay, I know that it's hard for you to imagine if something like this will happen to your online business. But if it's possible, try requesting a visit to the order fulfillment facility if they allow you to do it. At least it will give you a brief idea on their capacity when it comes to processing orders for your online store.

6. What are their procedures and policy for order fulfillment service

All order fulfillment services have their own procedures. So, you need to be aware of how they do things. Doing so will make it easy for you to integrate your procedures with their procedures. Most large order fulfillment services want you to follow their procedures. But lesser known and small order fulfillment services will do what they can to fit your business.

Large order fulfillment services usually don't want to work with start-up companies. They want you to be familiar with your customers' expectations. And they also assume that you don't have large sales volume.

7. What payment method they accept for paying your order fulfillment bills

Most order fulfillment services will bill you on a monthly basis. And the bill consists of their service charge and the shipping charge for the items. For the most part, they usually accept credit card payment. Some of them also offer other payment methods such as checks and bank transfer. If you prefer other types of payment method, you should ask them before you sign the agreement.

List of order fulfillment services

These order fulfillment services are based in the United States. But then again, you can still use it even if your business isn't based in the United States. Here are some of the order fulfillment services you can consider for your online store.

1. Order fulfillment by courier service

Couriers such as FedEx and DHL also have their own order fulfillment service. Unlike other order fulfillment services, you can only use their own courier service. They may only allow you to use another courier for shipping to countries they don't cover.

From what I see, their order fulfillment service is available worldwide. But the type of services will differ from country to country. If you know that they have such services in the US, the same service may not be available in your country. So, you need to check their website specific to your country to learn more about this service.

2. Fulfillment by Amazon (FBA)

Amazon isn't just a place for you to buy what you want. But they also provide you with order fulfillment service as well. All you need to do is to send your items to Amazon Fulfillment Centre. And they will process the shipment for you when they receive orders. If you're selling on Amazon, your products are also eligible for Amazon Prime FREE Two-Day Shipping, FREE shipping, and other benefits.

While FBA is for Amazon sellers, they also provide Multi-Channel Fulfillment service. This service allows you to fulfill orders from other channels. It can be your website and other marketplaces such as eBay. They can also process the returned items for you at any time.

The rate for FBA will depend on what items you ship, per customer order handling fee, pick and pack fee, weight handling fee, and storage fee. They also have a different rate for Multi-Channel Fulfillment as well. You can use their profitability calculator to estimate the amount you have to pay if you use FBA.

What's amazing about FBA is Amazon will handle everything for you. They will do the packing, delivery, customer service and returns. You only need to pay for the storage and the orders they fulfill, with the cost of shipping included in your fees. You can still use FBA if you live outside of the United States. But you need to read the FBA term for international seller carefully before you sign up. You need to have Amazon Seller account before you can use FBA.

3. Shipwire

Shipwire has everything you need when it comes to fulfilling orders on your behalf. It has everything you need just like what FBA offers. But what makes Shipwire above FBA is that they also provide other services such as custom packing lists, invoices and labels, custom packaging, marketing inserts and samples, relabel and repack services, kitting and virtual kitting and branded customer communications.

If you're thinking of expanding your business through dropship, Shipwire can also do it for you. The only thing you need to do is to get people to join your dropship program. And Shipwire will do the rest for you and your retail partners. With over 154 fulfillment centers in 45 countries, it's no wonder that Shipwire can do this on the larger scale.

The only way for you to get the pricing for their order fulfillment service is to send them a quote. So, the pricing will vary, depending on the scale of your business. Shipwire doesn't say anything about not catering to the start-up companies. But it doesn't hurt for you to get a quote from them. At least you can compare their pricing with other order fulfillment services.

4. Rakuten Super Logistics (RSL)

Rakuten Super Logistic (RSL) is formerly known as Webgistix. RSL doesn't just offer fulfillment service for your online store. But they also have e-commerce freight services. With this service, they will pick up the shipments from your suppliers. And they will send them to your RSL fulfillment centers. If you find it a hassle to deal with your suppliers and you want a lower freight cost, consider using this service.

Unlike FBA and Shipwire, RSL only has warehouses in the United States. They have warehouses in New York, Las Vegas, Atlanta, Reno, Scranton, and Austin. But then again, you don't have to be based in the United States just to use their warehouse facilities. After all, the only thing you need to do is to integrate their system into your online store. And they will pick up from any location in the world and deliver them to any destination.

Their system only allows a direct integration through API. So, you can only integrate with RSL if you use Shopify, Volusion or BigCommerce. As for WordPress e-commerce plugin, you can integrate RSL with WooCommerce. I'm not sure if they allow integration with other WordPress e-commerce plugins. But you can contact their support to find out more if they allow integration with other plugins.

Like Shipwire, you can only get the pricing for their service when you request a quote from them.

5. eFulfillment Service (EFS)

What I love about EFS is they don't have setup fees, no integration fees, no minimum order requirements, no hidden fees, no long-term storage fees and no long-term contracts. Like RSL, they also encourage you to use their preferred carrier. If you do, you'll get a freight discount of 70% for shipping into their fulfillment center. Their customer service team will also work closely with you to set everything up.

Like Shipwire and RSL, you can only get the pricing for your online store when you submit a quote to them.

Chapter Recap

Consider using order fulfillment service if you receive a large number of orders. And you can't fulfill them all by yourself anymore. Different order fulfillment service has a different procedure. So be sure to discuss with them if you have any concern or special needs for your business.

CHAPTER 17

Marketing Your Online Store

You already work so hard to create your own online store. It's not easy, but you've made it. Suddenly, the idea of marketing your online store seems terrifying to you. I hate to break the news, but the notion 'build it, and they will come' doesn't work at all. It doesn't matter how gorgeous or sophisticated your online store is. No one will come to your online store if nobody knows that you exist.

If you're worried that you look like a sleazy car salesman when you market your online store, then fret not. There are many ways for you to market your online store. Some of them are free. But it takes time to build momentum for your online store. If you want a faster traction for your online store, then you have to spend the money on advertising.

You don't have to do everything that I outline here. You only need to pick which one you think you can do and have the budget to do so. Let's take a look at the strategies for marketing your online store.

Email marketing
If there's only one thing you can afford to spend, then it has to be email marketing. It's because email is still the best way to communicate with your customers. People tend to engage more with emails compared to social media. Not only that, email stays with you regardless of the changes in trend and social media algorithm.

The best part about email marketing is it doesn't cost a lot of money to get started. In fact, some email marketing solution has a free tier which is perfect for those who are just starting out. If you have a list of customers who have bought from you in the past, you can add their email address. You can email them to let them know about your new online store and other promotions you currently have.

Email marketing is also perfect for getting potential customers to shop with you too. You can offer an enticing incentive to get them to join your mailing list. Offering a free discount coupon is a good incentive to get them interested. And it doesn't cost you anything to create this incentive. Unlike your existing customers, it takes a while to persuade them to shop with you. And it still takes time for them to start buying from you even if you already give them a discount coupon.

It's not that hard to get started with email marketing. Here's a few email marketing platform that you can use to get started with email marketing. You can pick whichever you think that will work best for your online store.

1. MailChimp

What I love about MailChimp is how well it integrates with WooCommerce and other apps. With MailChimp, you can use it to notify the customers about the abandoned cart. You can also use it to recommend products as well. Want to keep in touch with your customers? You can do that by automating the follow up to re-engage your customers. You can even welcome new customers with a note to introduce them to your brand and your products.

MailChimp also has a predicted demographic feature. This feature allows you to get a rough idea about your customers. When you know more about your customers, it will be easy for you to tailor your marketing message. You can also segment your list, so then you can create a marketing message relevant to that segment only. Like most email marketing platform, MailChimp also has a detailed reporting.

Keep in mind that some of the e-commerce features are paid features. It only costs $10 per month if you have less than 500 subscribers. MailChimp also has Forever Free plan. This plan allows you to have up to 2000 subscribers and send emails up to 12,000 emails per month. MailChimp also has pay-as-you-go option. You'll receive 300 email credits if the prepaid amount is $9. If you want more email credits, then you have to pay more.

MailChimp is the email marketing platform I currently used in all my websites. I also integrate MailChimp with the sample store as well.

2. MailerLite

MailerLite works the same like MailChimp. But what I love about MailerLite is it includes popup subscribe forms and a landing page. They even have these features in their Forever Free plan as well. If you've been using a separate app for these features, you no longer need them when you use MailerLite.

MailerLite doesn't have a direct integration with WooCommerce. So, you won't have the fancy pro features like the one you can get in MailChimp. But you can use WordPress plugin if you like to integrate MailerLite with your online store. Their Forever Free plan allows up to 1000 subscribers. But unlike MailChimp's Forever Free Plan, they have an autoresponder feature.

MailerLite is perfect if you want a free tier with an autoresponder feature. Autoresponder emails are common in many blogs. So, I've yet to come across any online stores utilizing the autoresponder feature. Perhaps your online store will be the first one to make full use of it?

3. Mad Mimi

Want to create a beautiful-looking email newsletter without tinkering HTML and CSS? Then Mad Mimi is perfect for you. It also has WooCommerce integration. But then again, it doesn't have fancy features like the one you can get in MailChimp. The pricing for the basic plan starts at $10 per month if you have up to 500 email subscribers. But they also offer a free plan where you can have up to 100 email subscribers and send out unlimited emails.

4. Aweber

Many people that I know are using Aweber as their email marketing software. What make Aweber stands out is because of its stylish sign-up forms. Well, I admit that they do have stylish sign-up forms since MailChimp sign-up form is ugly. And it's still the same even until today. If you want a nice looking sign up form, you have to use a third party app.

Aweber also has a direct integration with WooCommerce. But it can only add subscribe options at the checkout page, though. Aweber doesn't have a free plan. But you can test drive it for 30 days to see if Aweber is a perfect fit for your business or not. The basic plan starts from $19 per month for up to 500 subscribers.

5. Constant Contact

Constant Contact also provides a landing page for capturing the email address. But what makes the landing page provided by Constant Contact different is it has a specific role. Let's say you're giving a discount coupon for those who are joining your mailing list. You can then use a landing page that will allow the subscribers to receive an email with the coupon code on it. They also have other landing pages for event marketing and answering surveys as well.

But you can only get these features if you opt for their Email Plus tier, though. The price for Email Plus starts from $45 per month, and their Basic Email tier starts from $20 per month. Like Aweber, Constant Contact doesn't have a free tier. But you can try it free for 60 days to see if it suits your business or not.

They also have many integration and apps to choose from. But they don't have a direct integration with WooCommerce. They only have a direct integration with Shopify, BigCommerce, and Volusion.

6. GetResponse

GetResponse is email marketing software that has a close resemblance to MailChimp. But the only e-commerce feature they have is the abandoned cart email. Other than that, MailChimp still wins when it comes to e-commerce capabilities. But unlike MailChimp, it also provides landing page and a pop-up subscriber form. GetResponse also has a direct integration with WooCommerce too.

You can only get the abandoned cart email

feature if you opt for its Pro tier, which starts from $49 per month. Their basic tier doesn't have the abandoned cart email feature. And it starts from $15 per month for up to 1000 subscribers. They also provide a free trial too if you'd like to give GetResponse a try.

Search engine optimization (SEO)
If you want your customers to find you online, then you need to optimize your online store for the search engine. That's what it means with SEO. You're optimizing your site with the keyword phrase that your customers use online.

While optimizing your online store for the search engine seems hard, I can assure you that it's not as hard as it looks. What you need is the keyword phrase that has a lot of traffic but with less competition. After that, you can use the keyword phrase to optimize your online store. WordPress plugin like Yoast SEO can guide you on doing SEO for your online store.

The downside is it can be hard to find the keyword phrase that brings lots of traffic but with less competition. Fortunately, you don't need to do any guesswork to find a keyword phrase with such criteria. There's a tool out there that you can use to make it easier for you to learn more about the keyword phrase you choose.

1. Google Keyword Planner

Google Keyword Planner is a keyword research tool for finding the right keywords for display ads, search ads, and video ads. But you can still use it for research purposes. This tool will provide insight on the amount of traffic for that keyword, how competitive is the keyword and the cost-per-click (CPC) for that keyword. Not only that, but it will also give you information on other similar keyword phrases too.

The tool itself is free to use. But you need to have Google account before you can use it. You don't even need to add your credit card either.

2. Market Samurai

Market Samurai is a paid keyword research tool. What I love about Market Samurai is it also identifies if the keyword phrase is a profitable keyword or not. Their calculation is based on the CPC for the keyword times the number of traffic. Keep in mind that the profitability of the keyword won't matter much if you set the rule to long tail keyword phrase. But it's great to see that the long tail keyword can also be a profitable keyword as well.

Market Samurai costs $149. But if you buy it within the trial period, you only need to pay $97. It's the keyword research tool I currently use to find the keyword phrase for my websites.

Blogging

Blogging can be a powerful way to get exposure for your online store, especially if you combine it with SEO. If you know your target audience, then it won't be hard for you to come up with engaging blog posts for your blog. You can also use the blog as a way for you to engage with people who are on your mailing list.

Blogging can be time-consuming to some of us. So, if you feel that you don't have the time to update the blog, commit yourself to update the blog at least once a month. If you think that you can commit to blogging frequently, you can then choose to update the blog every week. Keep in mind that it takes time for the blogging effort to pay off. But you can only see the result when you update the blog on a consistent basis.

You can also choose to hire a freelance writer to write on your blog. But if people already know about you, keep in mind that they expect you to be the one who will write on the blog. They will consider buying from you after knowing you through the blog post.

Social media

What's the best place to build awareness for your online store other than on social media? If you think that social media sites like Facebook and Twitter are only for posting personal updates, then you're wrong. Sure, many people use social media for a personal reason. But it can also be a powerful tool for getting exposure for your business.

There are some businesses that I come across only from Twitter itself. I don't think I'll realize their existence if it's not because of Twitter. Sure, I may or may not buy from them. But if I ever need something, then their online stores will be the first one that pops into my mind. Do you want the same for your online store too? Of course, you do!

As a retailer, you don't have to use every social media channels available on the planet. If you think that your target customers are not there, then you don't have to be there. Like any other websites, these channels are only appealing to a certain demographic. If you already know your target customers and where they usually hang out, then you have to be where they are.

Social media marketing is a huge topic on its own. So, I will only give you a brief idea on how to make full use of these social media channels.

1. Twitter

You have no idea what's so appealing about Twitter. Well, how in the world can you convey your idea in 140 characters? From the business perspective, you need to be creative to convey your message in a simple manner. Because of its characters' limitation, you need to be straight to the point. And you have to include a clear call-to-action in your tweets. It can be a link to your product page or a link to the blog post if you have a blog.

You can also add photos in the tweets. According to Linchpin SEO, tweets that have pictures in it have two times more engagement than tweets with no pictures at all. Want more exposure? Don't forget to add a hashtag to your tweets. Tweets that have hashtags in it receive two times more exposures than tweets with no hashtag at all.

There are many things you need to know when it comes to using Twitter to market your online store. But what I write here is already good enough for you to get started.

2. Facebook

Many people love to use Facebook not only for keeping up with their friends and family. But they also use Facebook to keep up with their favorite brands. So, it makes sense for you to have a presence there. Chances are your target customers are most likely using Facebook too. With so many people are using Facebook, you don't want to miss this chance of bringing exposure to your business.

Unlike Twitter, you need to create Facebook page if you want to market your business. While Facebook page no longer work like it used to be, it can still bring exposure to your business. You may not be able to get the traffic on Facebook to get people to like your page. But having Facebook page does help with SEO. If you use the same keyword phrase as your site, the search engine will rank your Facebook page too.

But if you want to increase the number of people following you on Facebook, use Facebook ads. I will cover it later in this chapter.

3. Pinterest

Think Pinterest as a place for you to save your favorite pictures in categorized folders. But in Pinterest's case, the pictures that you pin from any website is called pin. And the categorized folders are called pinboards. Many people use Pinterest as a source of inspiration, reference, and even for shopping.

According to internal Pinterest data for 2016, 55% of people on Pinterest use Pinterest to find or shop for products. Not only that, 70% of incremental sales comes from new customers. So, what does it mean for you? It means that Pinterest helps with driving sales to your online store. And it also works if you're a brand new online store.

With Pinterest having such a tremendous potential for your online store, how you can make full use of Pinterest? First, you need to sign up for Pinterest for business. This account allows you to add your website link and access to your account insight. Don't forget to use Pinterest Rich Pins feature. This feature will provide the Pins with extra information right on the Pins itself. In this case, the Rich Pins will give you information such as the price of the item in real time, availability and where they can buy the product.

Since Pinterest is all about visual, be sure that your pictures are eye-catching. If you have a lifestyle photo showing your products in action, it will be even better. You can pin the pictures from your online store using Pin-It button or Chrome extension. You can also upload the picture and add the pin description and link to the product manually too.

You can use Promoted Pins feature to get more exposure for your online store. According to Pinterest, people who engage with Promoted Pins spend seven times more than people who didn't.

4. Instagram

Like Pinterest, Instagram is a great place for people to discover new products. As I write this, Instagram only begins to integrate the shopping experience recently. And it's only available to a group of iOS users in the U.S.

So, how does the shopping experience looks like on Instagram? Well, the look and feel of Instagram will remain the same. But you will have a tiny 'Tap to view products' label at the bottom left corner of the photo. Once the users tap the button, they will see the details about the product. The detail will include the price of the products and where to buy them. If they click on the product, they can view more information about it within the Instagram app itself. The users don't even need to leave the app only to view the product.

What if the users want to buy the product? They can tap the 'Shop Now' links that will bring them to the product page on the website itself. With this feature, you don't have to place the link in the description anymore. On Instagram, the link placed in the description isn't clickable at all. And you don't have to keep on changing the link in the profile to reflect the latest update on your website.

The feature is not yet available for all Instagram for Business users. But it's worth considering if you don't have a presence on Instagram yet.

5. Tumblr

Tumblr is widely known as a microblogging platform where you can post any content you want. So, in what way Tumblr can benefit your business, you ask? Well, Tumblr is also another way for people to discover new products too. But people can only discover the products if you put a tag in your Tumblr post.

Tumblr works the same like other blogging platforms. It's just that many people use it to create a short Tumblr post. Tumblr is perfect if you prefer to write bite-size content. Just like other sites, it can also give more exposures to your business as well.

Online marketplace

If you want to get a lot of exposures for your online store, you should sell some of your items in the online marketplace. Depending on the online marketplace, you need to pay a certain amount of fees to get your items listed there. Some online marketplaces only want you to pay the listing fee after the items were sold.

You can make a lot of money in the marketplace thanks to its high volume of traffic. But it's still not advisable for you to rely solely on the online marketplace. For one, you don't own the website. When you can't control something that you don't own, there is a chance that you may lose your business overnight. And it's only because they decide to change their terms and conditions.

It's hard to manage your presence in the online marketplace alongside with your online store. But you can use order management software such as Order Cup to manage the sales for all channels. Here are some of the online marketplaces that you can use for your business.

1. eBay

eBay is one of the most popular marketplaces. You can get everything you can think of, from beauty products to cars. So, it makes sense why many people love to shop on eBay. The good thing about eBay is anyone can begin selling there. And they also make it easy for you to get started with selling on eBay. You can also sell in their U.S site even if you don't reside in the U.S. But you won't be able to make full use of eBay feature such as printing the shipping label.

Listing on eBay is free for up to 50 items every month. If you exceed more than 50 items, then you need to pay 30 cents a listing per month. Once your items are sold, you need to pay seller fee which is 10% of the final price. If you need tools to list the items faster, manage your inventory and orders and track your sales, use Seller Hub. Seller Hub is free to use. You can switch back to the default selling tool if you don't like Seller Hub.

If you're making a lot of sales from eBay and want to add more items, then consider opening an eBay store. The basic subscription starts from $24.95 per month for 250 items. The eBay store can save you a lot of money if you list the item without using eBay store. Unlike the normal listing on eBay, the listing from eBay stores have lower seller fee which is 4% to 9% of the final price. So, the fee is more appealing if you have high sales volume.

Don't feel like managing the eBay sales on your own? You can use eBay Valet. It's like having a selling expert who will do everything for you, from taking photos to shipping out the products. What you need to do is to send the items to them, along with the prepaid shipping label. The only thing you need to do now is to wait for the cash to roll in. Keep in mind that they only allow certain items to sell through eBay Valet. So, you need to check first before using this service.

eBay Valet takes a certain percentage of your item's final selling price. The higher the price of the item, the more you earn. This service is only available in the U.S for the time being.

2. Amazon

Like eBay, Amazon is another place where people love to get their stuff from. The process of selling on Amazon is the same as on eBay. But some categories need approval before you can start selling on Amazon. And there are some categories that are available for Professional Sellers only.

You can choose to sell either as an individual or as a Professional Seller. If you plan to sell less than 40 items per month, then you only need to pay selling fees, which is $0.99 per item. You also need to pay other fees such as shipping fees, referral fees, and variable closing fees if you're selling Media products. If you plan to sell more than 40 items per month, then you have to pay $39.99 per month and other fees as well.

If you're using FBA to fulfill orders for your online store, you can also use it for the orders coming from Amazon. The fees for order fulfillment for sales from Amazon are much cheaper than order fulfillment for other channels, though. You can also fulfill the orders on your own if you want. But I suggest that it's better for you to use FBA, even for the international sellers.

You can sell on Amazon regardless of where you live. In fact, Amazon can pay you in your local currency too. It's too bad that only some countries can get paid through direct deposit. As for other countries, you need to use a service like Payoneer. If you're not familiar with Payoneer, think of it like PayPal.

With Payoneer, you'll get a US bank account, complete with details about your bank account. Besides US bank account, they will also provide you with a local bank account in GBP, EUR, JPY and CNY. With Payoneer, you can sell not only on Amazon US but also on Amazon UK, Amazon Europe, and Amazon Japan.

Payoneer only charges you 1% whenever you receive payment in USD. But there are no fees for receiving payments in GBP, EUR, JPY and CNY. From there, you can choose to transfer the funds to your bank account, even if it's in a different currency. Payoneer will only charge you up to 2% if you transfer the funds to your bank account. The charge applies to all Payoneer account in USD, EUR, GBP, and JPY.

If you prefer to have the funds accessible as a prepaid debit card, you can also apply to get one. It works the same like the debit card issued by your local bank. Keep in mind that you have to pay $29.95 per year for the annual fee, though.

3. Bonanza

Bonanza is formerly known as Bonanzle. In a nutshell, it's the alternative to eBay. It doesn't have as many traffic as eBay. But it's one of the places that you can try besides eBay. What I love about Bonanza is they will only charge you when your items are sold. They don't just charge you with the selling fees, but they also have extra charges if your shipping is more than $10. In this case, it can be hard for you to sell there if you live outside of the US and your customer base is mostly in the US.

Unlike eBay, there is no limit on how many items you can sell on Bonanza, even if you don't subscribe to their pro plan. Already have products on eBay,

Amazon, and Etsy? You can import your listing on eBay with Bonanza too, so you don't have to do the listing from scratch. You can even sync your listing so then there's no difference with what your customers see on your Bonanza booth.

Bonanza also provides a webstore like eBay store. But unlike eBay store where you can't customize the look of your store, you can customize your store in Bonanza. You can even use a custom domain if you want to. The basic plan starts from $20 per month. And they also provide free 14-day trial if you'd like to give their pro membership a try.

If you don't like the idea of signing up for the membership, you can make full use of their advertising feature. Unlike most advertising service, Bonanza will pay the advertising cost on your behalf. And they will only charge you the advertising fee after your product is sold. All you need to do is to pick which percentage of the largest fee you're willing to pay for your products.

4. Storenvy

Storenvy works the same like Bonanza. You can sell on a marketplace and through a customized webstore. But what makes Storenvy stands apart is its social community-driven aspect. Storenvy members can like the products and follow their favorite stores on Storenvy. From time-to-time, you can also take part in the promotion. If you're interested, you will only pay a certain amount of fee to get your item included in the promotion. But it doesn't end there. Storenvy will handpick and promote some of the products to their email subscribers.

Unlike Bonanza and eBay, your customers can use to pay either using PayPal or credit card when they buy from you. But you can only accept credit card payment if you have Stripe account, though. If you don't have Stripe account, then you can only accept credit card payment through PayPal.

What I love about Storenvy is they only take 10% of every sale you generate from the marketplace. And you'll keep 100% of the sales if you generate the sale from your webstore. There's no limit on how many items you want to list there. They also offer premium features such as using a custom domain and super discounts. You can also integrate your Storenvy store with the third party apps too.

I'm still selling on Storenvy even after I close down Fashion Paraizo. It's just that I no longer selling clothes. But I sell personal stuff instead. If you're looking for another place to expand your business, then you should give Storenvy a try. And if Storenvy does impact your business in a good way, feel free to contribute a few bucks to them. The money that you contribute will be used to make Storenvy better.

Pay per click (PPC) advertising
Did you notice that there are a few ads appear at the top of the search whenever you search for something on Google? Not only that, but you also notice that there are also a few ads on the right side of the search result. For those who don't know, that's PPC advertising.

It works by bidding on the potential keywords that your customers will use when they do an online search. When the keyword phrase they use matches the one you bid, they will see the ads displayed with the search result. The good thing about PPC advertising is you will only pay if someone clicks on your link.

The amount that you have to pay is depending on how much is the cost-per-click (CPC) of the keywords you use in your ad. So, the higher is the CPC, the more you have to pay. CPC is largely based on the number of search volume. So, expect to pay a lot if you're bidding on the keywords that have a large volume of traffic.

PPC advertising isn't the set-and-forget kind of

marketing channel. So, you need to track your ad spending while running an ad campaign. Otherwise, you end up spending more money than your ad budget. It's easy to overspend, especially if you're bidding a high competitive keyword. And it doesn't help that the traffic that you bring may not convert to sales.

Despite its risk, paid advertising is still one of the best ways to market your online store. Here are a few places that you can use to advertise your website.

1. Google AdWords

If you want people to see your ads on Google, then use Google AdWords. Your ad will appear whenever their search is related to your ad. You can use the same keyword you use to optimize your site as a keyword phrase for your ad. Doing so will help your site's visibility on Google.

2. Facebook Ads

Facebook ads aren't only for generating traffic to your Facebook page. You can use it to redirect them to your homepage or bring them to the landing page. Unlike Google AdWords, you can use Facebook ads to target specific audience. You can target your ads by the age, countries, and interest. If you know your target customers well enough, then Facebook ads will give you a better traction. After all, only people that meet the criterion will see the ads.

3. eBay Commerce Network

Just because you're using eBay's marketing solution, it doesn't mean that your ads will only appear on eBay. Sure, your ads will also appear on eBay. But at the same time, your ads will also appear on other websites such as Shopping.com and ShopStyle. In other words, eBay Commerce Network is a mixture of affiliate marketing and ad platform. In this case, you have other people who promote your products besides the paid ads.

The rate for the ads is still based on cost-per-click where you will only pay when someone clicks on your link. Anyone can use eBay Commerce Network to advertise. But if you're international seller, you can only use PayPal to fund your advertiser account. As for the US-based businesses, you can fund your account with a credit card.

4. Pinterest Ads

You can turn your pins into a promoted pin to get more people to your site. What I love about Pinterest Promoted Pins is that it's non-intrusive. After all, the

Promoted Pins look the same like the regular pins. So, Pinterest users won't feel distracted by the Promoted Pins when they browse the site. Using Promoted Pins will only make it easier for people to find the products that are right for them.

If you receive a lot of traffic from Pinterest, consider using Promoted Pins to get more sales. It's worth repeating here that people spend seven times more after seeing the Promoted Pins.

Shopping comparison sites
It's a website where you compare the price of the items that you want to buy from different retailers. Shopping comparison sites used to be one of the traffic sources for Fashion Paraizo back then. But after a while, it didn't seem to bring me any traffic anymore.

The rate is the same as the paid ads where the fees are based on the cost-per-click. You will only need to pay if someone clicks on your link. Unlike paid ads, people who are on that site will only click your link if they have an interest in your product. So, should you set aside the budget for the shopping comparison sites?

Well, it depends. If you're offering deals on a daily basis, then it's worth considering using it. But if you don't, then you should be spending the money elsewhere to attract more customers. If you rely on Google to drive traffic to your site, then you should also use Google Product Listing Ads as well.

Notice that there are items listed in Google's search results? Well, that's Google Product Listing Ads. With Product Listing Ads, your items will appear in the search result. And with other ads that are on top and the right side of the search result. If you'd like to see your items appear in the search result, then you need to create a product feed for your online store.

You can only submit it if you have Google AdWords account and Google Merchant Center account. Once you already create the account and verify the link, you can now begin creating the product feed. The process of setting up a product feed is rather tedious, though. You have to include every single detail about your products. And even worst, you need to do the same for the whole product listing. That is if you choose to submit all products to Google Product Listing Ads.

Be sure that your product feed follows the specification outlined in Google Merchant Center. Google will suspend your product feed if it doesn't follow the specification.

If you're using WooCommerce, you can simplify this process with the help of the premium extension. Now you don't have to worry about creating the feed manually and whether it meets the specification or not.

Affiliate marketing

Affiliate marketing can be a good way to generate sales with the help of affiliate marketers. Sure, you will only pay them when they're generating sales for you. But I will only recommend affiliate marketing to the established businesses, though. It's because it costs a lot of money. And you need a dedicated team to provide support for the affiliates.

If you have the capacity to manage affiliate marketing, then take a look at ShareASale. Upon signing up, they will guide you on how to create a successful affiliate program. But the cost of creating an affiliate program is $650 for the one-time fee. You also have to pay transaction fees where the fee is 20% of your affiliate sales. And also a minimum of $25 in monthly fees after activating the affiliate program for more than 120 days.

You can also choose to create your own affiliate program with the help of WordPress plugin. But then again, I can only recommend you to start an affiliate program once you have a dedicated team to handle it.

Chapter Recap

There are many ways to market your online store. But not all marketing strategies will work for you since it depends on your target market. So, you need to find marketing strategies that work best for your business.

If you can pick one, start using email marketing from the beginning. After all, it's the only marketing channel that you have a full control of. Keep in mind that email marketing is here to stay regardless of the trends.

CHAPTER 18

Outsourcing Tasks for Your Online Store

Outsourcing may not be something that crosses your mind when you're just starting out. Even if you don't need a full-time employee now, it's good to think about it at the beginning of your business.

Should you outsource works for your online store in the beginning?

I have nothing against outsourcing. Think of outsourcing like you're buying time for yourself. Sure, it's nice to have someone helping you with the daily operation of your business. But it may not be a good idea when you're just starting out. For one, you're not familiar with what you need to do for your online store. Not only that, you also don't have a consistent cash flow coming into your store yet. Without a steady cash flow, it can be difficult for you to pay them on time.

So, it's better for you to understand your business thoroughly before you hire someone to work with you. And it doesn't matter whether you want to hire a full-time employee or a freelancer. It's best to bring someone to work with you when you already have a full understanding of your business.

Keep in mind that it's okay for you to do everything yourself in the beginning. Most successful businesses start this way during the early stage of their business. But if you think that it's a must, then outsource something that requires a one-time payment. Things like setting up an online store using WordPress is one of them. The rest of the works require you to pay them monthly.

What tasks you should outsource for your online store

There are many tasks that you can outsource for your online store. These are some of the tasks that you can outsource, depending on what kind of online store you have.

1. Data entry job

A data entry job can be something like doing product listings for your online store. Your online store can't be empty with nothing to sell. So, you need to list what items you're selling in your online store. There are a lot of people who can do product listings for you. But if you have specific requirements, then you need to mention it in your job scope.

In my case, I need someone who has a basic knowledge of fashion and familiar with WordPress. I also did the same when I was hiring someone to do the data entry job for Fashion Paraizo. One of the criteria was they must be familiar with Volusion.

2. Order manager

This person will be in charge of managing your customers' orders. He or she needs to submit the orders to the suppliers if you are running low on stock. This person can also be answering the customers' queries besides your support team.

3. Bookkeeper

You don't need to hire a bookkeeper if you're only dealing with the online transaction. And you use bookkeeping software to keep track of your business income and expenses. But, if you're dealing with offline transactions most of the time, then you need to hire one. Be sure to have all documents ready to make it easier for the bookkeeper to do the bookkeeping for you.

4. Website maintenance

This person will do everything related to website maintenance. It can be updating the plugin, do backup for your site and troubleshoot any site problems. Like any technical job, you need to specify what this person needs to qualify for the job. In this case, you only want to hire someone who is familiar with WordPress.

5. Customer support

You'll never know what will happen in your business. It can be your shopping cart is not working properly, or your customers need your help. It's okay to handle the customer support yourself in the beginning. But it's better for you to have someone who can do this for you. Handling the support query can be draining to you, especially if you can't get the problem to resolve.

Things you should do before hiring employees
Before you begin bringing someone in your business, it's better for you to have these things ready. Sure, it can be tedious. And you may feel that these things are unnecessary. But then again, it doesn't hurt to have them ready. You'll never know that these things will come in handy when you need it the most.

Here are the things you need to have ready before you bring someone to join you. Not only it will save your time, but it can also make your business operation a lot smoother.

1. Creating training videos for training new employees
You already scout for the best talents. But that doesn't mean they're already familiar with your online store. And it doesn't matter even if they came from the similar industry like you. You need to create training videos to train your new employees about their tasks. The training videos will guide them to do things in certain ways.

Sure, creating training videos does take some time on your side. But in the long run, you don't have to explain the whole tasks again if you're hiring new employees.

2. Determine how you want to communicate with your employees

If your employees are working from home, then you need to have a way to communicate with them effectively. You can use Skype to communicate with your employees about their progress. But it's better to have a place where you can interact with each other. And also keep track of their job progress at the same time. You can use Slack and Trello to communicate and keep track of their progress.

3. Create access for your employees to access important documents related to your business

Be sure that all important documents are easy to access by your employees. Having these documents accessible for them is important. They don't need to email you back to back if they need anything. You can use Dropbox to store important documents and allow your employees to have direct access to it. You can revoke the access if they no longer work with you.

4. Prepare Non-Disclosure Agreement (NDA)

If your business deals with sensitive information, you need to have an agreement in place. Get them to sign

Non-Disclosure Agreement (NDA) to protect your business' confidentiality. With NDA, your employees will not share the trade secret to other people. That's always the case if they're working for your competitors after they quit working for you.

5. Give your new employees a trial period

I hate to break this news, but what they say in their resume may not turn out to be what you hope for. Well, I don't mean that they're cheating in their resume, hoping that they'll get the job. But when we see how impressive their resume is, we tend to have a high expectation on them.

Sure, some of them can be crème de la crème. And you feel lucky to have them onboard. Even if they happen to be a unicorn employee, it doesn't hurt for you to give them a trial period. The reason for giving them a trial period is simple. You want them not only to prove to you what they can do to your business. But they need to get themselves familiarize with your business environment and culture.

You don't want to bring people who don't fit into your business working environment and culture. You will only send them to destruction if you do that. It doesn't matter whether you're hiring freelancers or full-time staffs to work with you. You should evaluate them before you hire them. You can tell them that you'll be testing their skills for a period of time. And if you do it right, you will get the best employee that not only skillful but fits your company as well.

Where to find these people
Finding the right people for your business can be a tough one. And that's always the case if you want to hire someone who can fit into the company culture and environment. The last thing you want is the new employee who happens to be a toxic person and is affecting everyone in the office. There are a few places that you can use to find the best talent for your business. And what's the best part? You can find them online.

1. Post the vacancy on your website
If you want to find people who love what you do, why don't you just hire one of your customers to work for you? Not only they know what your business is all about, your core value and what you offer. But they're also a big fan of your business. You don't have to brief them about what you do and what you sell since they're already familiar with you. But you still need to train them and give them a trial period only

to see whether they're a good fit for your business or not.

Posting the job vacancy on your website is perfect for you if you prefer to work with the local talent. And you don't feel like paying extra for finding the right talent for your business. But keep in mind that you'll have to do everything on your own. And that includes interviewing the candidates and managing their payroll.

2. Upwork

Upwork is a website for you to find a range of top talent from around the world. With Upwork, you can choose to find and filter the talents yourself or post a job there. If you post the job, the freelancers who join Upwork will view your job post. They will submit their proposal to you if they like to take the job.

Of course, you can find out more about the freelancers who are submitting the proposal to you. You can schedule a chat if you want to know more about them. Already eyeing on the freelancers that you think a good fit for your business? You can contact them directly and see if they like to work for you. After choosing any of them, they will begin to work on your project and will deliver it to you during the deadline. You can opt to pay hourly or fixed rate.

If you don't feel like finding the talent yourself, you can then use Upwork Pro. With Upwork Pro, they will personally sort through the talent marketplace. And they will identify the best options for your tasks. All you need to do is to tell them what you need for your business. And they will come up with a list of possible candidates who are suitable for the task. Just pick from the list of potential candidates, and you're good to go.

3. PeoplePerHour

PeoplePerHour works the same like Upwork. The only difference is they're charging you fixed rate only. Besides the main service, they also offer more tasks for a specific rate if you need any of them. You can get pretty much done with PeoplePerHour, just like what you do in Upwork. But you can only use PeoplePerHour for one-time tasks instead of the on-going tasks. If you need someone for the on-going tasks, then it's better for you to use Upwork instead.

4. Fiverr

Fiverr is like PeoplePerHour except the task starts from $5. While the idea of paying $5 to do tasks for you seem like a heaven sent, keep in mind that it's only for the basic task. If you need someone to do a more complex task, you need to pay more. So, the total cost for the whole task will become more than $5. I use Fiverr when I need to outsource someone for a simple task.

5. Virtual Staff Finder
Unlike Upwork, Virtual Staff Finder is a place for you to hire virtual assistants (VA). The VAs are based in the Philippines. The hiring process is the same as Upwork Pro. You need to provide them with the description of the task. And they will find the right virtual assistants for you. You can also choose to interview them before you hire them. The only difference is you have to manage the payment to these virtual assistants on your own.

This service is perfect for you if you're looking for someone who wants to work full-time with you.

Chapter Recap
You need to consider outsourcing if you can't cope with managing the business operation on your own. Before you begin outsourcing the task, be sure that you have everything in place for the employees. You can hire a full-time employee or a freelancer depending on the tasks.

CHAPTER 19

Bookkeeping Simplified for Your Business

Bookkeeping may have been the dreaded word for you. And maybe it's the last thing you want to do in your business. Despite the dreaded feeling, you know that you need to do it for the tax filing purposes. It's true that bookkeeping is essential for tax filing purposes. But you can also use bookkeeping as a brief snapshot of your business.

Well, how are you supposed to know if your

business is making money or losing money if you don't do bookkeeping? Chances are, you may not know the state of your business if you don't do bookkeeping. Some of you may feel dreaded to do the bookkeeping because you feel that you're not good with numbers. But the good news is, there is a way to simplify the bookkeeping process and making it less dreaded.

That's when the accounting software comes in. And the best part, it will record every transaction once you already set the system in place. There are many accounting software to choose from. And some of them are widely used by many small and medium enterprises. Now you can say goodbye to painful and manual bookkeeping process.

1. QuickBooks

When you mention accounting software, QuickBooks will be the first software you hear. In fact, QuickBooks was the first accounting software that I came across back then. At that time, you could only get the desktop version if you live outside of the US. And the cloud accounting version of QuickBooks was only available in the US.

But now, QuickBooks Online are available in many countries. If your country is not available on the list, you can pick the International version instead. The International version is the same like the country-specific version. But the country-specific version will have a specific feature caters for that country. For example, QuickBooks Online for small businesses in Malaysia will have GST ready in it.

Have offline transaction? You can take a photo of the receipt and upload it on QuickBooks. You can even pay your offline invoices with QuickBooks too. Now you don't have to stash your bills in the shoebox. You also don't have to worry that you will lose the invoices for the tax-filing purposes. If you want to create invoices, you can do the same through QuickBooks. What's even better, you can do it from your computer or your mobile phone.

The basic version of QuickBooks Online starts at $15 per month. QuickBooks is also available as a desktop version. But they recommend you to use QuickBooks Online instead. The cloud version has better features than the desktop version. They also have a 30-day free trial too if you'd like to give QuickBooks a test run.

2. Sage 50

Sage 50 was formerly known as Peachtree. Unlike QuickBooks, Sage 50 is desktop-based software. But they also provide a secure online access too. Sage 50 has more or less similar features like QuickBooks. But it costs more than QuickBooks where the basic plan starts from $36.58 per month, billed annually. Like QuickBooks, there is also a country-specific version too.

Not only that, but Sage 50 also offers other add-ons such as Sage Payroll and Sage Payment Solutions. But these add-ons are only available for the US-based and Canada-based businesses only. If you're using WooCommerce, you can also integrate it with Sage Payment Solutions.

3. Kashoo

Kashoo is cloud-based accounting software like QuickBooks. Unlike QuickBooks and Sage 50, Kashoo is purely online-based accounting software. You can use it not only for keeping track of your sales and business expenses. But you can also sync your business bank account where it can sync more than 5000 banks worldwide. If you find that QuickBooks is hard for you to grasp, then give Kashoo a try. It's simpler than QuickBooks.

Kashoo only has one simple pricing, which costs $19.95 per month. They also provide 14-day free trial if you like to give it a try.

4. Wave Apps

It's like Kashoo and QuickBooks. But what I love about Wave Apps is their accounting software, and invoicing software is free. If you need to do payroll, you can use Wave Apps too. The cost for the payroll will depend on how many employees you have. And it's simple to set up too.

You can use Wave Apps regardless of where you live. But some services are only available in certain countries such as accepting credit card payment for invoice payment and lending service through OnDeck. For now, the lending service through OnDeck is currently available for the US-based businesses only. Other than that, you can use these services regardless of where you live.

You can also use Wave Apps for your personal finance too. It works the same like as business accounting software. Wave Apps is the accounting software that I'm currently using in my business.

Chapter Recap

Bookkeeping shouldn't be something that will make you cringe. With accounting software, you don't have to do manual bookkeeping anymore. Accounting software isn't only for recording your business transaction. But it can also provide you with a financial snapshot of your business. You can use this financial snapshot to come up with the best decision for your business.

BEFORE YOU LEAVE

Just like any other authors out there, I hope that this book can help you to get started with creating an online store on WordPress. After all, this book covers everything you need, from setting up your site to marketing your business. I admit that you may not be able to grasp everything in this book at first. But that's okay. What matters the most is you take that tiny, baby step to start creating the online store for your business.

But if you still feel overwhelmed with creating and managing an online store on your own, then fret not. I already create checklists based on what I write in this book. Unlike the book where I write based on the topic, the checklists are focusing more on the action-step instead. Rather than having you to figure out what next step you should take and the things you need, my checklists already covers everything you need. And that includes tutorial videos.

If you prefer to have something that complement this book in the form of action-step checklist, then take a look at my WordPress E-Commerce Blueprint Checklist Bundle. You can learn more about it here:

http://www.theefficientyou.com/checklist

SAMPLE STORE

As you already know, I already turned Fashion Paraizo into a sample store so then you can see for yourself how your online store will look like on WordPress. Of course, you may not be able to see the back-end side of the sample store. But at least this sample store can give you a rough idea on what to expect when you're using WordPress to create an online store.

Just to let you know that the sample store will not process any order at all. So, feel free to play around with it. If you'd like to have a look at the sample store, you can go right here:

http://samplestore.theefficientyou.com

RESOURCES MENTIONED IN THIS BOOK

Online store software
Self-hosted WordPress - http://www.wordpress.org

Domain registrar
Namecheap - http://www.namecheap.com
GoDaddy - http://www.godaddy.com
1&1 - http://www.1and1.com
Enom - http://www.enom.com
iWantMyName - http://www.iwantmyname.com

Hosting
Hostgator - http://www.hostgator.com
Bluehost - http://www.hostgator.com
Media Temple - http://www.mediatemple.com
SiteGround - http://www.siteground.com
WPEngine - http://www.wpengine.com

WordPress e-commerce plugins

WP eCommerce - https://wpecommerce.org

WooCommerce - http://www.woocommerce.com

MarketPress - https://marketpress.com

Jigoshop - https://www.jigoshop.com

Cart66 - https://cart66.com

Shopping cart plugins

Gumroad - http://www.gumroad.com

Selz - http://www.selz.com

Shopify Buy Button - https://www.shopify.my/buy-button

SamCart - https://samcart.com

Premium WordPress themes

WooCommerce - http://www.woocommerce.com

Elegant Themes - http://www.elegantthemes.com

Studio Press - http://www.studiopress.com

WPMU Dev - https://premium.wpmudev.org

Obox Themes - http://oboxthemes.com

Bluchic - http://www.bluchic.com

Theme Forest - https://themeforest.net

Online payment

PayPal - https://www.paypal.com

Stripe - https://stripe.com

2Checkout - https://www.2checkout.com
Paymentwall - https://www.paymentwall.com

Buy SSL certificate
Hostgator - http://www.hostgator.com
Namecheap - http://www.namecheap.com
GoDaddy - http://www.godaddy.com

Email client
Mozilla Thunderbird - https://www.mozilla.org/en-US/thunderbird/
G Suite - https://gsuite.google.com/

Customer support software
Olark - https://www.olark.com
Hosted Support - https://www.hostedsupport.com/

Premium WordPress plugins
BackupBuddy - https://ithemes.com/purchase/backupbuddy/
iThemes Security Pro - https://ithemes.com/security/

Order management software
Order Cup - http://www.ordercup.com/
ShipStation - http://www.shipstation.com/
ShippingEasy - http://shippingeasy.com/

Stamps.com - http://www.stamps.com/
ShipRobot - https://shiprobot.com/
Ordoro - https://www.ordoro.com/
Shippo - https://goshippo.com/

Customized, branded shipping boxes
Packlane - https://packlane.com
Lumi - http://www.lumi.com

Fonts, graphic, photography for the commercial use
Creative Market - https://creativemarket.com

Order fulfillment service
Fulfillment By Amazon (FBA) - https://services.amazon.com/fulfillment-by-amazon/benefits.htm
Shipwire - http://www.shipwire.com/
Rakuten Super Logistics (RSL) - https://rakutensl.com/
eFulfillment Service (EFS) - http://www.efulfillmentservice.com/

Email marketing software
MailChimp - https://mailchimp.com/
MailerLite - https://www.mailerlite.com/
Mad Mimi - https://madmimi.com/
Aweber - https://www.aweber.com/

Constant Contact - https://www.constantcontact.com
GetResponse - https://www.getresponse.com/

SEO software
Google Keyword Planner - https://adwords.google.com/KeywordPlanner
Market Samurai - http://www.marketsamurai.com/

Social media sites
Twitter - http://www.twitter.com
Facebook - http://www.facebook.com
Pinterest - http://www.pinterest.com
Instagram - http://www.instagram.com
Tumblr - http://www.tumblr.com

Online marketplace
eBay - http://www.ebay.com/
Amazon Marketplace - https://services.amazon.com/selling/benefits.htm
Bonanza - http://www.bonanza.com/
Storenvy - http://www.storenvy.com/

Pay-per-click (PPC) advertising
Google AdWords - https://adwords.google.com
Facebook Ads - https://www.facebook.com/business

eBay Commerce Network - http://www.ebaycommercenetwork.com/

Shopping comparison site
Google Product Listing Ads - https://www.google.com/intl/en/retail/shopping-campaigns/

Affiliate marketing
ShareASale - http://www.shareasale.com/

Outsourcing sites
Upwork - https://www.upwork.com/
PeoplePerHour - https://www.peopleperhour.com/
Fiverr - https://www.fiverr.com/
Virtual Staff Finder - http://www.virtualstafffinder.com/

Bookkeeping software
QuickBooks - https://quickbooks.intuit.com/
Sage 50 - http://www.sage.com/us/sage-50-accounting
Kashoo - https://www.kashoo.com
Wave Apps - https://www.waveapps.com/

ABOUT THE AUTHOR

Suhaili Shazreena used to be an online fashion retailer where she sells Japanese fashion brands on her website, Fashion Paraizo. After closing down Fashion Paraizo, she decided to share her experience in the online retail business through her book. Now, she's an indie author who shares her experience with self-publishing through her website, The Efficient You. Besides writing non-fiction books, she also writes fiction book under the pen name, Sekina Mayu.

Connect with me online

Website: www.theefficientyou.com

Twitter: www.twitter.com/theefficientyou

Books by Sekina Mayu

The Diary of Modern Cinderella

Twisted Destiny

Trigger Locked: The Mind Control Assassins

www.ingramcontent.com/pod-product-compliance
Lightning Source LLC
Chambersburg PA
CBHW030921180526
45163CB00002B/417